DESERT NEIGHBORS

Books by
Edith M. Patch

NATURE STUDY

Dame Bug and Her Babies

Hexapod Stories

Bird Stories

First Lessons in Nature Study

Holiday Pond

Holiday Meadow

Holiday Hill

Holiday Shore

Mountain Neighbors

Desert Neighbors

Forest Neighbors

Prairie Neighbors

NATURE AND SCIENCE READERS

Hunting

Outdoor Visits

Surprises

Through Four Seasons

Science at Home

The Work of Scientists

DESERT NEIGHBORS

by

Edith M. Patch
and
Carroll Lane Fenton

drawings by

Carroll Lane Fenton

YESTERDAY'S CLASSICS

ITHACA, NEW YORK

This edition, first published in 2020 by Yesterday's Classics, an imprint of Yesterday's Classics, LLC, is an unabridged republication of the text originally published by The Macmillan Company in 1937. For the complete listing of the books that are published by Yesterday's Classics, please visit www.yesterdaysclassics. com. Yesterday's Classics is the publishing arm of Gateway to the Classics which presents the complete text of hundreds of classic books for children at www.gatewaytotheclassics.com.

ISBN: 978-1-63334-081-7

Yesterday's Classics, LLC
PO Box 339
Ithaca, NY 14851

CONTENTS

CHAPTER I

VISITING A DESERT

WHEN you go to one of the deserts in our country, you may wish to stay for a long visit. When you think about it all afterwards, you may wish to go back—to see the brown mountains again and to take more walks across the reddish-buff sands. You will think how much you would like to become better acquainted with the birds, the little mammals, and the hungry lizards you saw during your first visit. It will be fun to learn more about the creatures that burrow underground. You will wish to see the plants again, too, even though many of them are so prickly that you need to be careful when you are near them.

You will feel that way about it because a desert is not a barren place where nothing—really *nothing*— grows. A few deserts do have bare hills, called dunes, made of sand that moves, or drifts, every time the wind blows. But even between dunes there are valleys where flowers bloom, birds nest, and Lycosa, the spider, digs her tunnels. You will expect to meet those spiny plants called cacti (or cactuses); but you may be surprised to find so many shrubs and to see trees as often as you do.

1

Are you beginning to wonder what a desert is? It is just a part of the country where very little rain falls. Sometimes whole seasons pass without any showers at all. In some deserts, several years may go by between really good rains. Then some of the plants die, but many of them manage to keep on living. They will grow leaves and flowers very quickly when rain falls on the land again.

Some deserts are so far north that snow covers the frozen ground in winter. Most of the plants in these deserts are small and bushy, with tough leaves. The sagebrush is one and the rabbitbrush is another. The cactus plants there have wide, flat joints and long spines; and they grow close to the ground. These are "prickly pears," but they are much smaller than their relatives that grow in deserts farther south.

Shall we walk across one of those southern deserts? We soon notice that the plants do not grow close together, like those of forests or swamps or meadows. Desert bushes stand far apart, with bare sandy ground between them. In most places the ground has no grass. When there is grass, it also may grow in small clumps or bunches.

There is no grass on the ground we see in the picture opposite, but a flat place not far away has some. If you visit that flat place in the evening, you may see some little kangaroo rats. They will be smaller than "Bannertail," who lives in a different desert. But they will hop on their long hind legs, just as he does, and will eat the ripe seeds of grass.

The bushes are scattered with bare ground between them.

Plants do not crowd one another in deserts, because there is not enough water during most of the year. But when enough rain falls in late winter or very early spring, thousands and thousands of plants sprout from seeds lying in the sand or from roots hidden underground. They grow very rapidly and bloom. Then the desert valleys and hillsides become bright with orange-yellow poppies, blue or purple lupines, and pink sand verbenas. The beautiful flowers do not last very long. When dry weather comes again, the gay plants wither in the sun. Then their stems are broken and blown away by the wind. It piles them in corners or covers them with sand, and the ground between the bushes is left bare again.

But never think that deserts become dull and tiresome just because the flowers are gone! There is a desert near the southeastern corner of California where you will see nothing but sky and sand, yet the wind has piled the buff sand into such stately hills that you will be very sorry to leave them. In another desert, where Chuck and Testudo live, you will find mountains of rock weathered into all sorts of strange and beautiful shapes. And if you go to the White Sands, in New Mexico, you will find a great deal to do and see—even at a time when the yuccas are not in bloom and the bushes have no flowers.

Of course, when you roam across the deserts, you will wish to see an oasis. There you will find springs of cold, good water that you will like to drink. Birds also drink it, and so do some other desert creatures. When the water seeps away through the sand, mesquite trees grow much bigger than they do in drier places.

Among them will be tall cottonwood trees, with thicker trunks and wider leaves than those of the cottonwoods that grow on prairies. And if the oasis you visit is one of the very best sorts of all, some tall palm trees will lift their fan-shaped leaves above both mesquites and cottonwoods. The picture below shows just such an oasis, where there are more than twenty palms.

Tall Fan Palms Growing in an Oasis

A Joshua tree is a member of the Lily Family.

On high slopes near the palm oasis you will see the strange Joshua trees. A great many of them grow in the valley at the very foot of the mountain where Chuck Walla lives. Joshua trees have large woody trunks with thick rough bark; yet they really belong to the Lily Family. Their greenish-white blossoms grow in large clusters. Each flower has six lobes, as do the flowers of their lily relatives. When you look at the delicate lilies in a flower garden, you may be surprised to think of their giant relatives—desert trees that sometimes grow to be about forty feet tall.

A Joshua tree is one kind of yucca. Yuccas have stiff, narrow, evergreen leaves with sharp, dagger-like points. It is because of these leaves that people call the yuccas "Spanish bayonets." The yuccas you will see in the White Sands are different from those in some of the northern deserts; and there are yuccas of still another kind growing in the Texas desert where Cornu, the horned lizard, lives. Some have strong, coarse leaves, and some have thin leaves the edges of which split into fibers that hang in long tatters. But they all have their leaves in crowded tufts at the ends of the stems or branches; and they all have their whitish blossoms in branched clusters at the tips of straight stalks. The flower stalks of some of the yuccas are very tall indeed.

Shrubs that are common in deserts can stand much dry weather because they have roots that reach far down through the sand for water. Among the shrubs you are sure to meet are saltbush, creosote bush, and sagebrush.

The saltbush has mealy, whitish, leaves with a salty

taste. Sheep like these leaves and eat a great many of them. The saltbush belongs to the Pigweed Family (also called Goosefoot Family). Like other members of this family, it has small, greenish flowers growing in little clusters.

A Barrel Cactus

A sagebrush, or wormwood, is not related to the true sages, which belong to the Mint Family, but it does have a rather sagelike odor. Its flowers are not pretty, and they have a lot of dusty, yellow pollen that is shaken out of them and blown about by the wind. But their grayish leaves and gnarled branches give sagebrushes a very attractive appearance and make the desert quite silvery.

The creosote bush is an evergreen shrub with a strong, though rather pleasant, odor. Its leaves are small and narrow, and the petals of its pretty little flowers are yellow and partly twisted.

In almost every desert, and in many places not quite dry enough to be true deserts, you will find the cacti. At first you may not like them, for they have sharp spines that hurt you if you put your hand on them. But after you learn to go near them very carefully you will probably decide that they are the strangest and most interesting of all desert plants. Even such names as barrel cactus, beaver tail, cholla (which is pronounced *cho-ya*), hedgehog, prickly pear, sahuaro, and staghorn, will make you wonder how they look.

As you may know, leafy plants depend on the green material in their leaves for their lives during their growing season. All these plants need sugar for food. It is the green stuff in their leaves that makes their sugar for them. The leaves are really sugar factories that work all day in the sunlight but cannot work at night. Cacti need sugar too. They have no useful leaves, but they keep the same green material in their stems. So their

The Cholla in which Yodeler and his mate built their nest.

sugar factories are in their stems. (Some cacti have tiny leaves on their youngest joints.)

The thick stems of cacti also serve to hold their water supply. After rains, cacti take in water with their roots and store it in the pulpy part of their stems. At such times the ridges in the tall stem of a giant cactus (or sahuaro) look plump. In a long drought, however, the plant uses so much of its water supply that the ridges become shrunken and thin.

You will meet many cacti in the desert and see the pictures of some of them in this book. Which will you like best? Perhaps the cholla, in which cactus wrens often build their nests. Perhaps the giant cactus where Gila woodpeckers dig their home holes. Since a cactus of this sort sometimes grows to be thirty-five or forty feet tall, these birds can have homes far from the ground.

Plants change from season to season; and even the desert itself changes as year after year goes by. Rocks crack, wear, and begin to crumble into grains of sand. Strong winds move the sand from place to place, piling part of it in heaps about shrubs. It is such mounds that kangaroo rats, and pack rats too, often seek when making their homes.

The winds do not always blow the sands in straight processions. Sometimes they go in whirlwind parades. Then the wind, and the soil it carries, whirls round and round, or twists. A whirlwind may be a little "twister" only a few feet high, or it may reach up in a tall whirling pillar like a small tornado.

Crota's home among red stones which are broken parts of petrified trees.

There are certain deserts where the sands are not all one color—not all light brown like those in Testudo's home, and not all white, like the gypsum in the White Sands. There also are deserts where there is more clay than sand, and the clay may be colored red, pink, brown, buff, and greenish, as well as several shades of gray. There are bright deserts of that sort in southern Utah. There is another beautiful one in Arizona. Nearly four hundred years ago, an explorer gave this desert a Spanish name that means the same as our words *painted desert.* It is on a hill just south of the Painted Desert that Crota lives and suns himself beside red stones that are bits of petrified trees. Some of his relatives live in the Painted Desert itself, and so do relatives of Shorthorn, the horned lizard you will meet in the third chapter.

When you go to the desert, don't stop for a day

and drive away. And don't make your home in a hotel. Take a tent and camp beside tall cacti or among gnarled mesquite trees. You may expect it to be a very quiet camp—but probably you will be surprised. Cactus wrens will sing all day and Gambel quails will call *kurr, kur-kurr!* Bees will hum among mistletoe flowers. Doves will call *coo, coo, coo-oo-oo.* At sunset, crickets will start to chirp, and you will hear the thump of Jack's feet as he hops about in search of supper. Here and there a sleepy bird will twitter, and you may hear faint little chirps made by Bannertail and his neighbors. Then a desert fox will call *yap, yap!* making Bannertail hurry into his burrow.

If you are very lucky, a coyote will sit on a hill while he sings to friends far away on the desert. His song will start with a few barks; then it will rise in a high howl and end with several sharp yaps. It will surprise you and perhaps frighten you a bit at first, but soon you will begin to like it. As you listen to the song some night you will be glad when another coyote answers. After you have left the desert, one thing you will wish to go back for will be to sit near a cactus in the moonlight and hear a coyote sing!

CHAPTER II

BANNERTAIL, WHO HOPPED LIKE A KANGAROO

THE August moon rose while Bannertail waited in one of the doorways of his home under a mesquite tree. He had lived in this home for a long time—ever since one summer night more than a year ago.

That was an exciting night: Bannertail was making his first visit to this part of the valley. He had wandered over from another place in the desert and was having a good time hopping here and there while he looked about. Then a hungry desert fox suddenly chased him, and Bannertail hurried into the first hole he found. He stayed there, hidden and quiet, until the fox became tired of waiting and trotted away.

The hole into which Bannertail rushed when the fox startled him was a long tunnel, or hallway, in a strange house. Soon after the desert fox left, Bannertail began to go slowly through this house. It had a mound of sand, almost four feet high, for its upper part. Under the mound were many halls that led down into rooms deep in the ground. Bannertail met no other little animals as

Desert Scene near Bannertail's Home

*The August moon rose while Bannertail waited
in one of the doorways of his home under a mesquite tree.*

he went along these sloping tunnels. No one had been living in the house for many weeks. Some of the walls had crumbled and the place was not very tidy.

Still, Bannertail liked the empty, tumble-down house where he had found safety in a time of danger. He cleared out some of the rubbish that was in the way. Then he dug a place the right size to use for a bedroom. There were too many doorways opening outside to please him, so he plugged all but six of them with sand. Some of the rooms were good for storerooms. In these he began to put piles of food on the floor.

16

That August evening when the moon came up, Bannertail was thinking about grass seeds, good to eat, that were ripe enough to carry to his storerooms. When seeds were ready to harvest, he worked part of every pleasant night.

He was a bit timid as he came out to the roof of his mound house into the moonlight. He had never quite forgotten that there were foxes in his desert world. So he paused for a few moments to look with his big eyes and to listen with his round-rimmed ears.

Bannertail's body, sand-colored and white, was nearly as large as a rat's; but he was much prettier and daintier than a rat. His nose was pointed like that of a mouse and his whiskers were slender and sensitive. His long furry tail ended with a fluffy white tuft. While he waited outside his door, Bannertail sat on his big, strong hind legs, bracing himself with his tail which was stretched out behind him. His front feet did not touch the ground. They were very tiny, and he held them tucked up under his chin except when he needed to use them for hands.

This little creature really was a relative of rats, of mice, and of squirrels, but he did not act like these relatives when he traveled. If you could have seen him that night when he started off for his load of grass seeds, you would have laughed. He went with kangaroo jumps, hopping on his hind legs. At first he took rather short, slow hops and looked carefully about as he went. But soon he quickened his pace and was leaping three feet at each jump; and his tail stuck out in the air, with its tuft of white fur making a flag, or banner, behind him.

You can easily understand why little animals of this sort have been given rather queer names. They are neither rats nor kangaroos; but they are called "kangaroo rats," because they look a bit like rats and travel like kangaroos. Some people call them "bannertails," a quite good name for them, too.

As Bannertail went across the desert sand, he followed a narrow path, or road. He had made it himself, by hopping that way many times. It ran straight from his home to some grama grass whose tops were filled with yellow seeds. When he came to the grass, Bannertail stopped and filled his pockets with the seedy tips.

Bannertail's pockets were two fur-lined pouches, one on each side of his face. When they were full, he looked as if he had the mumps!

When his pouches could not hold another grass seed, he hopped back along his path and dodged through one of his doorways into a long tunnel. The tunnel was dark, but he moved quickly, going round corners and through more doorways. Perhaps his long whiskers were a help to him and kept him from bumping his nose. As soon as he reached a storeroom, he emptied his pouches by pushing against them with two jerks of his front paws, or hands. Then he hopped away for another load.

While he worked, Bannertail listened. Though the desert seemed peaceful, there were creatures living there who would like a kangaroo rat for supper. Once an owl flew overhead—and Bannertail kept so very quiet that the hungry bird never guessed he was not just a part of the sand. Far away a fox barked—and Bannertail stopped gathering grain till he knew that the fox was not coming toward him. While he waited, he made a thumping sound by hitting his heels against the ground.

Bannertail had a habit of thumping like that when he was alarmed and nervous and ready to run away. It may be that the other kangaroo rats, who were gathering seeds near by, heard the noise of his heels or felt the jar of the ground. Perhaps Bannertail's thumps seemed like a danger signal to them. Some of the other kangaroo rats began to thump on the ground in the same way. Had they been warned by Bannertail's nervous heels? Or had they, too, heard the distant fox barking?

The creature that surprised Bannertail most that night was a coyote. He came so silently that the kangaroo rat, busy with his harvesting, did not notice him until the wolf was very close. Then Bannertail jumped straight up into the air, leaving the coyote right *under* him, snapping at the ground where Bannertail had been a moment before. More quickly than the coyote could look up, Bannertail was on his way. After taking a few jumps five or six feet long, he came to a burrow near a cholla cactus. He did not try to go home—that was too far away. He escaped by darting into this near burrow, which was so deep and long that no coyote could dig him out. Bannertail hid there until long after the wolf left that part of the desert; but after a while he recovered from his fright and went home.

One fall night, when Bannertail's storerooms were nearly full, he left his home to *play*. His leaps were as long as those he had once taken to escape the coyote, but this time he was jumping with joy. He came to a bare, dusty spot under a mesquite tree and began to hop up and down there as if he were trying to reach a leaf that dangled from the tip of a low branch.

While Bannertail played, neighbors joined him. In a few minutes there were six happy kangaroo rats near the mesquite tree. One hopped round and round in circles on the sand, another jumped back and forth over tall grass tops, while the others took long running leaps. They frolicked together like the best of friends.

Suddenly, Bannertail left his comrades. He felt hungry and hopped to a place where he had once found some extra good seeds. He seemed to know just where to go, but when he got there he took little hops among the desert plants and smelled of different seed tips, seeking those he liked best. While he was hunting, three neighbors came. They hopped and sniffed, too, often coming close to Bannertail. For about five minutes he did not object to their company; but after he found the seeds he wanted most, he stopped being friendly. He began to pack the favorite food into his pouches; and every time another kangaroo rat hopped too near, Bannertail jumped over him and kicked. His neighbor had to dodge very quickly to avoid being hit by Bannertail's heels.

One night, on returning to his home after such an evening of fun and feasting, Bannertail found

The coyote who tried to catch Bannertail.

something that made him angry. It was the track of Buff, going into Bannertail's door. Buff was a kangaroo rat but not of the same kind as Bannertail. He was much smaller and lighter colored. He lived not far away under an ocotilla. (An ocotilla is a spiny desert shrub with very tall, slender, upright stems and splendid scarlet flowers. Another name for it is "candlewood.") Buff's house had plenty of long halls, but it was not very large and had no big rooms to fill with seeds. He gathered some food for himself; but when he wanted a lot to eat, he went where he could get it most easily—to the pantries of his bigger and busier relatives. Just then he was in one of Bannertail's storerooms stuffing his pouches as full as he could while the owner of the house was away.

When Bannertail came home, Buff suddenly found himself in trouble. Two powerful feet hit his back and he was pushed out of the room in a way that made him know he was an unwelcome guest. He dodged into a tunnel, dropping the seeds from his pouches as he went. Bannertail followed him, kicking him several times before he reached the door. It was a very scared and sore little Buff who hurried out of the house and hopped down one of the roads that led from Bannertail's home.

For many weeks before Buff's visit, the weather had been dry and the sky had been sunny by day and starry by night. Then, a few days after that event, the sky became dull and cloudy. The first of the rain fell in a fine misty drizzle. A little later came flashes of lightning and rumbles of thunder, while the rain poured down in what is called a "cloudburst." The storm filled the great dry arroyo, or gully, with a muddy river and sent

Bannertail's Mound House

a sheet-flood over one place where Bannertail liked to gather seeds. Fortunately for him, the water did no real damage to his house, for it did not flood his tunnels and soak his storerooms.

Bannertail stayed indoors during the rainy day and all through the cool wet night that followed. He slept most of the next day, which was cool and drizzly. At sunset he went to the door, looked out, and returned to his comfortable, dry tunnels. The damp sand did not interest him. He did not even care to go to a puddle for a drink of water.

Rainy weather kept Bannertail in his house; but cold nights did not bother him. Even when a chilly wind came from the north, freezing some of the prickly-pear joints, Bannertail went out as usual. When he did not wish to gather seeds, he played, hopping up and down by himself until his neighbors came to join him in some jumping game.

One night in the midst of a frolic, Bannertail saw something strange. It was a tin can dropped by people who had been having a picnic on the desert. He stopped jumping and turned his back to the shining object and kicked. *Spat, spat!* went the grains of sand as they hit the tin. Bannertail looked to see what would happen. Would the queer thing run away? When he found that nothing happened, he came closer and kicked more sand at the can. Still the can paid no attention to him, so he kicked again. After that he put his head near enough to sniff at the tin. Deciding that it was not good enough to eat, he hopped lazily away.

As he hopped, he found some bits of bread left by the picnickers. He kicked sand on them. As they did not run away or turn to fight him, he nibbled one piece and found that it had a pleasant taste. He tucked the other pieces into his pouches and carried them home. It was time to go to bed for the day, in his nest far down at the end of a long winding tunnel. But first he would put the bread into a storeroom. It would be very good to eat for his luncheon when he was hungry.

CHAPTER III

THE HORNY ONES

CORNU

CORNU was lucky. It was now October, and no one had taken him away from his desert home. A great many things had happened to him since he awoke from his winter's sleep last March, but all had ended pleasantly for him.

One day early in the spring of that year, a boy called Bob had picked him up near a road and carried him to his father.

"Daddy," Bob said, "look at the Texas horned toad I found. When he tries to get out of my hands, I just tickle him on top of his head or under his chin, and then he stays as quiet as if he were tamed!"

Was the queer little creature that Bob cuddled in his hands really a toad, as many people call him? Did you ever see a toad with scales on his body and claws on his feet? Well Cornu had scales and claws. Then, too, when Cornu had been quite young, even on his very first day, he looked about like his father and mother except that he was tiny. He never had a tadpole babyhood, such as frogs and toads have—with a shape quite different from those of his parents. No, Cornu was not a toad. He was a *lizard*.

Bob played with Cornu for a while and then said, "I like him. He's comical. Shall we take him home for a pet?"

"If you like him well *enough*, Bob," answered Father, "you will let him stay in the desert. Horned lizards can be kept alive in zoos where they are given all they need— just the right temperature and plenty of proper food. But in people's homes, like ours, they usually die after a few weeks or months."

Bob decided that he liked Cornu "well enough" to let him live in the desert where he belonged. But he did not think that the little lizard was safe near a road where many travelers passed. Perhaps someone would find him there and take him away from the hot climate that agreed so well with him. So Bob carried Cornu to a place where few people cared to go, and put him down in the sand beside some tall yucca plants.

The next morning Cornu waited a while where Bob had hidden him, blinking in the sunshine. The sun would need to warm his body before he could move quickly enough to catch any insects for his breakfast.

Cornu had not had many breakfasts that spring. Indeed, only a few days before, he was lying in a dark hole, where he had been since sometime in November. The hole had been started by a mouse, but Cornu made it bigger and deeper to fit his own body. Then he lay

A Texas Horned Lizard

still and went to sleep. His eyes shut, his body grew stiff, and his legs stuck out awkwardly. Now and then, but not often, he took short, jerky breaths which showed that he was still alive.

At last the spring sunshine warmed Cornu's hole. His body stopped being cold and stiff, and his eyes began to open. One afternoon he wriggled his legs and crawled to the surface of the ground. Soon he was spry enough to walk and to catch a small black beetle that ran across the brown sand near him.

If you were as small as that beetle, Cornu would look very big to you: big and very, very fierce. Yet he measured only about four inches from his nose to the tip of his tail. His tail was stubby, and his body was wide. His short legs could run quickly for a dash of a yard or so, but they could not go fast very far.

Why did he look so very fierce? Because he had a great many horny spines. Some of them stuck out behind his head, others were arranged in two rows on his sides, while many covered his back and tail. They made his brown and buff skin rough. They also helped him to look like the bare ground as long as he kept still. Of course, nothing can look like ground while it moves its head or wriggles or runs.

There were some brownish-red ants near the yuccas where Bob had left Cornu. After eating a few of these, he rambled about until he came to a regular ant path which ran among small clumps of grass. This path was used by harvesting ants, and Cornu stopped beside it and waited for something to come.

Soon he saw two ants, each carrying a grass seed. First Cornu stood almost on tiptoe, head high and tail twitching. As the ants came near, down went Cornu's head and out shot his sticky tongue. He swallowed the first ant with a gulp and hurried to catch the second. Then he returned to watch the path. Cornu caught fifty or sixty ants before he was ready to leave this good hunting place and take a nap in the sunshine.

A few mornings later Cornu found a new ant path and began to catch another breakfast. But just after he took his first ant, a brown beetle crawled into sight. Cornu turned his head to watch, twitching his stubby

*The Yuccas, or Spanish Bayonets,
beside which Bob put Cornu.*

tail. Then he raised himself high on his front legs and leaned forward. He put down his head and thrust out his tongue. The sticky tongue pulled the beetle off the ground, but not quite into Cornu's mouth. Cornu jumped back, puffed his body out and seemed to wonder, "What will you do now?" The beetle started to walk away, so Cornu followed it for several feet, scrambling over sand and pebbles. Then he caught it with his jaws (not his tongue!) and managed to swallow the big mouthful. That beetle contained more food than several dozen ants and was worth the extra work of catching it, even though its shell-like skin was hard and its feet scratched him as he gulped.

In May, Cornu met his mate. She was larger than he was, and her back was lighter. The spots behind her head were a chocolate brown, and the spines on her sides were light yellow. She was really just as good-looking as Cornu, even though her complexion was not so dark.

Mr. and Mrs. Cornu played a great many games of tag under the creosote bushes. They also dodged round the long, sharp-tipped leaves of yucca, or "Spanish bayonet." They never seemed to hurt themselves on the hard points of the "bayonets," or to get stuck on cactus spines or torn by mesquite thorns. Yet any person who had tried to catch them would have got some very bad pricks.

Both Mr. and Mrs. Cornu liked to play and hunt for ants late in the morning. Some horned lizards of other kinds who live in drier, warmer deserts like the hottest part of the afternoon a great deal better. Cornu and his mate did not know anything about their relatives, but they did feel too lazy, during hot afternoons, to do much more than rest in some safe, shady corner.

One day Cornu's mate did not wait to play with him but ran away by herself. She went to a dry, bare hillside and began to dig a small hole. She scratched the dirt loose with her front feet and pushed it away with her hind ones. When the hole was seven inches deep, she laid six yellowish eggs, each about one-half inch long. Then she packed dirt around them, laid six new eggs, and covered them with dirt. She kept busy in this way until she had four layers—twenty-four eggs all tucked away. After filling up the nest, she went hunting for ants and caught a beetle or two besides.

As she went back down the hill, something swooped over her head. Mother Cornu stopped and puffed out her body, but she did not need to be afraid. The hawk had seen what she was and he knew too much to eat anything as spiny as that. To be sure, Churca, the road runner, might have captured her; but even that lizard-eating bird would not have swallowed such a spiny head as this horned lizard had. (Churca sometimes ate less spiny horned lizards.)

It was one day in July that Cornu climbed that same hill. He was wandering toward a sunny slope where there were flies to catch. On the way, he stopped to see what was wriggling in the sand. The ground stirred and heaved while he watched—and out came two dozen soft brown things that looked very much like Cornu himself. Why not, since they had just hatched from eggs that Mother Cornu had laid seven weeks before?

But Father Cornu did not understand that these tiny horned lizards were his own children—each looking as he had looked two years ago. As a matter of fact, they did not even interest him, now that he saw that they were nothing he cared to eat and nothing that would hurt him. He merely turned away from them and went on up the hill to a place where some flies were sunning themselves on little gray and white stones. Flies, now, were much more important to him than his family—for he was hungry and these insects would make a very good luncheon.

The next twelve weeks were rather quiet ones for Cornu. Then, one day in October, he had a really exciting adventure. As he walked down a trail he met a stray, hungry, ranch dog. The dog pushed Cornu with his paw, but he seemed afraid to bite. He would not like to get those horny spines into his mouth.

Cornu puffed out his body, lowered his head, and ran toward the timid dog. The dog backed away but stuck out his paw and barked *"wow!"* very sharply. He felt a bit braver after he had barked, so he put his nose rather close to Cornu and sniffed. That sniff was too much for the lizard. His neck grew stiff, his eyes swelled and bulged, and he made a hissing sound. From a corner of each eyelid went jets of blood that hit the dog in the face. By that time the dog had had enough of horned "toads," and dashed off down the trail as scared as if he had met an enormous foe—instead of a little puffed-up lizard. Cornu lay quiet for two or three minutes and then went to hide under a prickly-pear cactus. There he rested an hour or so before going off to catch bees or ants for luncheon.

SHORTHORN

Shorthorn was a relative of Cornu, for she was a horned lizard, too, though of a different kind.

Shorthorn lived in a valley far from the home of Cornu and his mate. The valley is between high mountains with pine trees growing on their slopes. The climate in this valley is so mild that Shorthorn could live in the open almost until Christmas. She could come out of her hole earlier in the spring than Cornu—while he still was stiff and chilly. That gave her more time to hunt and eat, or to sleep under the prickly chollas, in whose branches cactus wrens like to nest.

Shorthorn

Shorthorn was bigger and darker than Cornu, and she had shorter horns on her head. Her back had black blotches and big brick-red spots, and the sides of her face were dark pink. She had only one row of spines on each side, where Cornu had two.

She was different from the Cornus in another way, too. As you will remember, when Mother Cornu was ready to lay her eggs, she put them in a hole and pushed dry dirt over them. Shorthorn did not lay her eggs at all, but kept them inside her body while she slept, caught ants, and snapped at grasshoppers. Then, one day in the first week of August, thirty baby Shorthorns were born—or really *hatched* inside their mother.

CHAPTER IV

PEP WHO WORE
A SHINING ROBE

A GLOSSY bird flew to the top of a scraggly old mesquite tree and perched near the tip of a branch. He held his head high and lifted his crest and sang.

There was much of elegance in Pep's appearance. His graceful, slender body was clothed in shining black feathers that gave blue and green reflections. On his wings were white patches that showed when he flew. His glistening crest added to his beauty, and his eyes gleamed like red jewels.

If you look in a bird book, you will find that the names of a bird of this kind are *Phainopepla nitens*. The first name, *Phaino-pepla*, is made from two Greek words—one means *shining*, and the other means *robe*. The second name, *nitens*, is Latin for shining. So, in English, his name is "Shining-robe shining." The man who chose these Greek and Latin names certainly wished us to know that birds like Pep have really glossy feathers! Since these learned names are rather long, perhaps you will not be sorry we use a nickname and call the bird in this chapter just "Pep."

Pep lifted his crest.

There was a reason why Pep was happy enough to sing when he came to the mesquite tree. Long stems of mistletoe hung from the mesquite branches like tangled tassels. On these dangling stems were many reddish berries, and Pep liked red mistletoe berries—liked them, perhaps, better than any other fruit. So of course he sang!

Are you surprised to learn that Pep's mistletoe berries were red or pink, instead of waxy white like those you often have seen used for decoration at Christmas time? Well, you may be surprised, too, to know that the stems on which they grew had no yellowish evergreen leaves like those of that white-berried mistletoe. Indeed, they had no leaves at all—merely little greenish scales.

Leafless mistletoe, of this kind, thrives on mesquite. It grows also on cat's-claw, paloverde, and several other desert trees. It pushes its root tips, or "sinkers," into branches and lives on the sap these trees provide. Like other mistletoes, it is a shrub that cannot get its own food from the ground. The berries of this desert mistletoe have a good flavor—such a very pleasant taste, indeed, that people sometimes gather them to make jelly.

Pep ate these delicious berries for breakfast, for dinner, for supper, and for luncheons between his other meals. Because they were rather sticky, he often wiped his bill by scraping it on a mesquite branch. In this way he sometimes left seeds where they could grow into new clumps of mistletoe. Of course Pep did not know that he was a gardener, planting mistletoe seeds!

Reddish berries grew on these swinging mistletoe stems.

When the supply of mistletoe fruit ran short, Pep ate some other berries that he found near his edge of the desert. He also ate small insects when he could find them flying about. Some of these insects visited the mistletoe blossoms for pollen or nectar. Indeed, Pep really was one of the birds known as fly snappers—only you may be sure people added "shining" when they spoke of him, and called him the "Shining Fly Snapper."

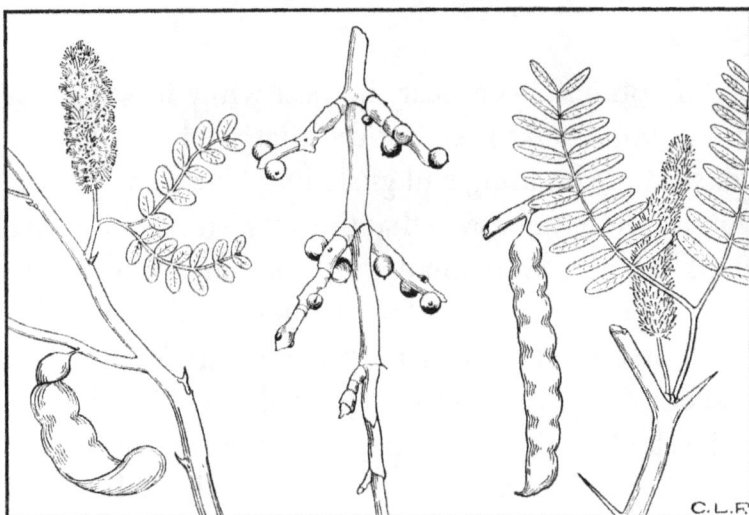

Some Plants that Pep Used: Cat's-claw, Mistletoe, Mesquite

When Pep snapped at a fly, or other small insect, he hovered, with fluttering wings, while he reached up in the air and caught it. If the insects were close together, he would poise in nearly the same place while catching a dozen or more before he went back to his perch. He could do other flying tricks, too, when he felt like showing off.

One day, rather early in the spring, Pep dashed about in a reckless sort of way and turned a somersault in the air. Then he strutted along a mesquite branch and sang a tune that sounded about as gay as his somersault looked. That was the day when he tried to make Miss Pep gaze at him and think him the very smartest bird on the desert. He was not disappointed. Miss Pep did like him very much indeed, and became his mate. Soon, of course, they looked about and chose a place for their nest.

If you had been near the nest while it was being made, you would have noticed that the bird who did most of the building had glistening black feathers. So you would have known that this was Mr. Pep; for Mrs. Pep's feathers were shades of gray and brown. She brought a short twig, a few slender dried stems with old blossoms at their tips, a piece of shredded bark, a stalk of dry grass, several sagebrush leaves, and some cobweb fibers, but Mr. Pep did not seem to be glad for her help. He seemed to wish to bring all the building materials, himself, and fit them into their proper places.

The nest, a soft-webbed, gray affair, rested on a fork of a mesquite branch just above a clump of mistletoe. Mrs. Pep left an egg in it soon after it was ready for her, and the next day she put in another. Two eggs were all she laid, though sometimes birds of this sort lay three. The eggshells would have been pale if they had not been so speckled; but no egg could seem very light-colored with several thousand dark dots on it! Since each of Mrs. Pep's eggs was only about seven-eighths of an inch long, you may be sure those speckles were tiny.

Father and Mother Pep took turns sitting on the eggs for thirteen days and nights. On the fourteenth day the twin Peps hatched. Then their parents had a busy time feeding them until they were old enough to pick their own berries and catch their own small insects.

When Sonny Pep and his sister began to fly among the mesquite trees, what sort of neighbors did they meet?

In that part of the desert, there were wood rats with white throats; and they were busy in as many interesting ways as were Albi and Gula whom you will meet in another chapter. But the young Peps knew nothing of the "packing" and "trading" and other doings of the wood rats. Indeed, it is quite likely that they never even saw those little creatures of the night-time.

Of course there were plenty of lizards, of one kind or another, roaming about on the sand or darting among the creosote bushes. They did not creep up the mesquite trees to feed on mistletoe berries, nor bother the Pep family in other ways. So the young birds paid no attention to their lizard neighbors.

Many of their bird neighbors, though, they must have noticed at one time or another. Red-winged blackbirds, in singing flocks, rested on the mesquite branches for a short time twice a year—when they were journeying northward in the spring, and when they were moving south in the fall. They were only visitors.

All the year through, the desert quails were near. The Peps heard them calling *"kuk"* and *"qua-ale"* and

This Gambel's quail was one of Pep's neighbors.

"whay day!" They saw them scurry under the lower branches of the mesquites when they wished to hide.

Mesquite Tree with Bunches of Desert Mistletoe

If these handsome quails, with long black head plumes, had done nothing but hide and call, or walk on the bare ground, the Peps would not have cared at all. The Peps did not object, either, when the quails dined on grasshoppers and ants or lunched on the seeds of grass or desert flowers. But when these birds came to the mesquite branches and began to feast on mistletoe berries, Father and Mother Pep both felt so cross that they scolded the quails. What did the quails do then? They calmly went on swallowing mistletoe berries until they were quite ready to leave. So far as they could see, they had just as much right to this fruit as the Pep family had!

Some cactus wrens had their own ideas about the way a mistletoe clump could be used. In that neighborhood there was no cholla cactus in which to put their big nest. But that really did not prevent them from making their home there. Indeed, they found that a large tangle of mistletoe was a perfectly good place in which to build. And they were quite, quite sure that they owned all the mistletoe stems that dangled round their nest!

Sonny Pep and his sister were not interested in what wrens and quails thought about their neighborhood. As they grew up they shared the feelings of their parents. A place with plenty of mesquite trees draped with the stems of leafless mistletoe was a jolly good home—for Peps who wore shining black robes and for their brown and gray mates.

CHAPTER V

ALBI AND GULA

ALBI, a pack rat, was mending his house. It was old, and some of the rooms were tumbling down. Every day or two part of a wall would crumble, and Albi would hurry out for something that would do to stuff into the hole. He would often come back with creosote twigs or a joint of cholla cactus. Repair work was not a new job for Albi. He had been at it, off and on, ever since he and Gula, his mate, first built the house.

They had built it under a big clump of prickly-pear cactus, where thousands of long, sharp spines kept hungry coyotes away. Those spines did not bother Albi and Gula at all. They had a way of their own of creeping among them without even pricking their feet or stabbing their sides. That was pleasant, for they liked prickly pear to eat. Whenever they felt hungry, they stopped working on the house, climbed part of the cactus, and nibbled its big juicy joints.

Gula and Albi started their house by digging a hole about a foot deep among the roots of the prickly pear. This was the beginning of their basement. They cut twigs from creosote bush and mesquite, carried them in their mouths, and piled them on the ground above the opening of their basement hole. Then they brought fallen branches of cholla, the thorniest cactus on their desert, and piled them on top of the sticks. After four or five weeks, they had one big room with its floor on the ground and two attic rooms above it. From the outside, this house looked like a pile of cactus joints, sticks, dry weeds, and other rubbish, tangled tightly together.

Sometimes Albi and Gula went into the basement to dig in the sandy ground. After they had been working on the house for two months or so, they had several tunnels. The dirt they brought up was dropped through the loose walls of the house. It helped to make a good foundation for the rough, spiny part above ground.

Just as the building seemed to be done, Albi started additions and repairs. When the sticks and cholla joints settled and became packed more tightly together, he piled new ones on top. Some tunnels were too narrow to suit him, so he and his mate dug them wider, or even turned them into rooms. Every month, the house became bigger, safer, and stronger—both above and below the ground. From the way Albi and Gula toiled, you would think that their walls never could tumble down.

Still, they did not look like hard workers. Their graceful bodies were clean and their fur was fluffy and pretty. Their backs and heads were rich gray; the fur on their sides was tinted with buff. Their feet were white and so were their under parts, including their throats

Albi enjoyed a luncheon of prickly pear.

and the under side of their tails. Their whiskers were very long and black—though some of their own kind in other deserts had whiskers that were almost colorless. From their noses to the tips of their tails, they were almost twelve inches long.

While the house still was being built, Gula began to carry grass into the first, largest room on the ground floor. She made a tangled ball of the grass which she mixed with long, thin strips that she chewed from creosote bushes. The ball had a hollow center for a nest, and she lined that with fur. Some loose fur she pulled from her own body, and the rest she picked up from sticks and cacti where she and Albi had lost it while they were working.

One night, after a supper of prickly pear, Gula went into the nest and stayed there. The next morning two tiny pink and gray babies lay with her in the middle of the round ball.

Like many mammal babies, these were born with their eyes closed. They had to drink milk instead of eating food of any other kind, and they were not able to walk. Unlike most babies, they were not willing to stay alone, even when they were asleep. They held to their mother very tightly with their mouths when she tried to go away.[1]

Gula loved her babies very much—but she simply could not stay at home with them all the time until they

[1] Baby bats cling to their mothers, too. Perhaps you may like to read about their habits in "The Bat, a Flying Mammal," a chapter in *First Lessons in Nature Study.*.

were old enough to run with her. She needed food, and Albi did not bring her any. She needed more than usual, indeed, since she must make milk for her hungry twins!

What did Gula do? As soon as the babies were strong enough, she let them keep their good tight holds of her while she crawled out of the nest. She walked across the large room and out through a cactus-lined tunnel. Then she hopped to the roof of her house and ran to the tip edge of a prickly-pear joint. There she sat down to eat as fast as her paws and teeth would let her.

But the babies? What happened to them? Oh, they were quite all right. Though their mother had dragged them all the way, they were perfectly comfortable. On their backs, they slid along the floor of the living room, through the cactus-walled passage, over the rough roof, and among the sharp prickly-pear thorns. Not a single spine hurt their soft little bodies, just as not a single spine pricked their mother's tender feet!

When the twins were almost grown, and had been running about and feeding themselves for a long time, neighbors moved under a big cholla not very far away. They began to build a cactus house of their own. Often they nibbled the "meat" from one end of the fallen joints of the spiny cholla. But they also liked prickly pear. Rather than go a longer distance for it, they visited the cactus near Albi's home and stayed for breakfast or supper.

Instead of chasing these neighbors away, Albi and Gula were friendly. Sometimes they came out with the twins to play or eat with their new friends. Perhaps all six would be eating at once, each perched on his own joint of prickly pear.

Albi ate the flat, juicy joints of a prickly pear cactus.

Not long after that, some people camped among the yuccas not very far from Albi's home. The place seemed so pleasant and interesting that they put up an olive-green tent and decided to stay two whole weeks. There was no water near their camp site, but what of that? They could bring all they needed in special heavy linen bags from a spring several miles away, at the very edge of the desert.

On the first night the people were there, Albi and Gula visited their camp. Albi was carrying a piece of cactus to add to the roof of their house, while Gula had a short stick in her mouth. But when Albi saw an empty tin can, he dropped his cactus and took the can. Gula left her stick on a table, and picked up a shiny knife that someone had forgotten to put away. Later, Albi came back, dropped a small red stone, and carried away a cake of soap.

Before the people finally pulled up their tent pegs and went away, tin cans, knives, soap, and dishcloths were tucked among the cactus joints and sticks that made up the two mounds where Albi and his neighbors lived.

You can understand why the people in the tent called Albi a "pack rat." He carried, or "packed," things away, whether he needed them or not. He could not eat the cake of soap, and the shiny can at the top of his house was not good roofing material. But Albi found it a pleasant game to drop one thing and pick up another, and he liked the looks of the tin well enough to spend almost an hour dragging it across the sand.

Sometimes the pack rats took things too big for one to drag or carry. Gula found a loaf of bread one night which was six times as big as she was. Albi and the two neighbors helped her pull and push; so the bread rolled over the desert until the busy little animals found something else they would rather "pack" away.

Other people called Albi a "trade rat" because he often left something in place of the article he carried away. Of course Albi did not "trade" in a business way, as people do. He merely dropped whatever he had when he found something he liked better. That was all he did when he "traded" the red stone for a cake of soap.

Still another name for Albi is "wood rat." This seems a queer name for a desert animal, but he has relatives who build their houses on the ground among the trees in forests, and they were given this name first.

Do three names seem enough for one little creature? Not quite. Albi has a more formal name which you may see printed in some books. This is *Neotoma albigula*. We found this rather a long one to use for the pair of wood rats in this chapter. So we called them "Albi" and "Gula" for short. Since the word *albi* means *white*, and *gula* means *throat*, do you think they are good enough for nicknames? These small animals really are white-throated wood rats, you know.

CHAPTER VI

A DESERT TORTOISE
AND HIS NEIGHBORS

TESTUDO

Testudo, a desert tortoise, was resting beside a small gray smoke tree when a hungry coyote found him. A moment later, the coyote's teeth closed upon the edge of Testudo's thick, hard shell, but they could not bite through it. They merely left scratches on its surface. Then the hungry animal tried to nip Testudo's legs; but these were so tightly tucked inside the shell that the coyote could only scrape the tough, horny, platelike scales with which they were covered. Nor could he reach Testudo's head, which was withdrawn into his shell even farther than his feet.

Luckily, the coyote did not happen to turn Testudo over on his back and gnaw at the edge of the under plate of his shell near one of the hind legs. If he had done this and had gnawed long enough, he could have wounded Testudo. But, just as he was becoming discouraged by the hard shell that protected the tortoise, a jack rabbit leaped by a creosote bush a few rods away.

The coyote at once lost his interest in Testudo and dashed off to try his luck with a breakfast that wasn't hard-shelled. Whether the coyote succeeded or not, Testudo never knew. All he cared about was to be left alone and undisturbed.

To be alone and undisturbed—what more could a desert tortoise ever need to keep him contented? Well, plenty of food, of course, and plenty of drink!

Desert tortoises, to be sure, can go a long time without eating and still not starve; and they can exist a much, much longer time without water and keep perfectly healthy. Indeed, some people who are fairly well acquainted with these interesting reptiles think that they never need any water at all, except what is contained in the juicy flowers and leaves they eat.

Did Testudo really like water? Yes, once in a while! Once in a very long while! And, as he had not had a drink since he awakened that spring, he may have felt a bit sluggish while he waited beside the smoke tree after the coyote left him.

The air above the desert became sultry that spring day. By early afternoon a fluffy cloud appeared in the west, and an hour later the whole sky was covered with great clouds that were very dark. Thunder rumbled and lightning flashed; then rain began to fall in big splashy drops. Soon the raindrops were coming down so fast that mud slopped against Testudo's shell. Water ran down every arroyo, wearing the steep banks away and carrying along the sand and even large pebbles. Broad thin sheets of muddy water crept across even the almost

The smoke tree beside which Testudo rested.

*An arroyo is a flat-bottomed gully. Its steep banks
are worn away by water, after storms.*

level slopes. The whole desert became wet and muddy
because of that quick, hard rain.

After the storm ended, as suddenly as it had begun,
Testudo started to walk across the wet sand. He swung
his front legs in a queer manner as if he were swimming;
and stepped on tiptoe, the five claws on each front foot
rattling faintly against the pebbles that they touched.
There were only four claws on each large hind foot,
which he brought down upon the ground flatly instead
of on tiptoe.

Testudo was an old tortoise, almost a foot long.
The curved shell that covered his back and sides was
brown and yellow, with many lines and ridges arranged
in attractive patterns. The nearly flat underpart of his
shell was yellow. This part of a tortoise's shell is called
a "plastron." (*Plastron* is a French word, meaning

breastplate.) Testudo's breastplate had a deeply notched lobe that sloped up under his neck. There was also a notched rear lobe that stuck out under the base of his tail.

The old desert tortoise waddled along until he came to a pool left by the rain. There he stopped and poked his head and neck into the water. This was his first drink of the season, and he swallowed an astonishing amount of water. At last he was satisfied. If he didn't have another drink until the fall rains came, he could live and not be weak or ill; but *if* there were some pleasant midsummer showers, he might welcome a drink then, too.

Following the spring rain, the appearance of the desert changed. Seeds sprouted and the new plants pushed their stems up through the sand and blossomed. Shrubs put out fresh leaves and flowers.

Testudo often rested as he waddled across the pebbly sand.

Testudo went where the growth was plentiful and tender. So did every other tortoise in that region. You would have been amazed at the number of big, little, and medium-sized Testudos that came from bare places in the desert to nibble juicy leaves and stems and blossoms. There was such a large party of tortoises that you might think they were having a picnic.

But even at this gathering, the tortoises had very little to do with one another. For the most part, each attended to his own feast and paid no attention to the others. When two males met, however, there was likely to be a fight; for this was the mating season as well as the time of the spring banquet. During the mating season tortoises are as ready to fight as are the antlered wapiti,[2] although they are not so noisy about their duels.

Testudo, himself, had two fights. The first one was when he met a big muddy male who stopped squarely in his path. Each of them nodded a few times; then they stepped backward several feet and drew their heads part way under their shells. After that they ran clumsily toward each other, bumping the curved points of their breastplates. They repeated this performance a number of times, but neither of them was really hurt and they soon turned aside and waddled away. Testudo's next fight ended in a different manner. After running to bump the other male, Testudo tucked the front lobes of his breastplate under the upper shell of his rival and flopped him over on his back. There he lay, waving his four legs in the air, while Testudo went off and enjoyed a luncheon of tender buds.

[2]"Cervus the Bugler," a chapter in *Mountain Neighbors*.

Hardshell, Testudo's mate, was a large old tortoise who was not more sociable than he. After spending a few days with him near the banqueting place, she went back into the desert alone. When her eggs were ready to be laid, she put them in a hole she dug in the sand. The sun warmed them for about ninety days before they hatched, and neither Mother nor Father Testudo was anywhere near the sandy nest at that time.

Testudo once had had a good home. It was a burrow more than six feet deep in the sandy bank of an arroyo. The heavy rain, however, had washed away this home, and the banks were hard places in which to dig. Testudo found a knoll under a big creosote bush and used his flattened front feet as shovels. The opening of his new burrow looked like a small badger hole, a little wider at the lower edge than at the curved top. He dug, deeper and deeper, pushing the sandy soil out with his shell and rough shoulders. The clumsy tortoise worked slowly, but he finally finished a satisfactory dugout.

All the time that he was digging he had nothing to eat. After the one big rain, weeks before, there was not even a shower. Leaves on the saltbushes became dry, some of those on the mesquite trees shriveled and fell, and even the creosote bushes turned brown. Testudo did not nibble at them. He did not like hay and dry fodder as did a cony, or pika.[3] He wanted his leafy salads juicy.

Since there was nothing outside that interested him, Testudo crawled into his new home one evening just as

[3]"The Little Haymaker," a chapter in *Mountain Neighbors*.

the stars were showing. At the bottom of his hallway, he turned round and shifted until his shell and legs seemed to be comfortably placed. Then he drew in his head and went to sleep. He still was sleeping next morning, and he dozed all that afternoon. In fact, he might not come out again till another rain fell on the desert, causing some plants, now dry, to be fit to eat.

GRID

When Testudo did come out of his hole one morning, something jumped up in front of his nose. It scampered swiftly across the sand, with its showy black and white tail sticking up in the air. Near a saltbush, it stopped as suddenly as it had started and at once seemed to look like the ground on which it rested. Testudo could not see where it was, and he didn't care enough to try to find it. But a hungry hawk, sailing overhead, did care—yet he could not see it again, either, though he gazed and gazed.

This successful hider was Grid, whose name was Gridiron-tailed Lizard. (Some people call him Zebra-tailed Lizard.) Grid had a cream-colored head and a throat that was white with gray shadings. On his brownish-gray back were many white spots, while his sides and legs were tinged with pale yellow. Close behind each front leg was a blue-green spot between black wedge-shaped marks which were trimmed with rich, bright orange. His slender, pointed tail was white with dark bands which were widest and blackest near the tip. He was almost ten inches long.

Like many other lizards, Grid could change his colors. While staying on very light sand, much of his skin would be pale. If he remained in the shade of a bush, his back would turn a darker gray. Such changes helped the lizard to hide, because his colors resembled those of the pebbles and the desert sand. But often he would wave his tail over his back, showing his black and white bands plainly. At such times he might easily be seen by a leopard lizard or a hungry hawk. After displaying his tail in one place, however, he would dash off to a different place and really hide—this time keeping his tail quite still when he stopped. The showy bands on his tail may be spoken of as "flash colors." Whether or not his flash colors were a benefit to him, Grid certainly made many, many successful escapes.[4]

Grid was hungry that morning when Testudo alarmed him by coming out of his hole. After remaining quiet for a time, he curled his tail up over his back again and ran to a place where beetles were crawling among dry leaves and fallen twigs at the foot of a creosote bush. Grid cocked his head and leaned forward: in a few minutes he had snapped up four brown beetles. He did not get the full flavor of these insects, for he swallowed his food whole. How could he really chew, with teeth that were only tiny points?

After eating all the beetles he could find among the leaves, Grid darted off to some ants that were crawling out of their home, carrying grains of sand. He gulped

[4]If you care to read more about "flash colors" and how they are displayed, you may find an account of them in "Safety First, among Animals," a chapter in *The Work of Scientists*.

them down as fast as he could, for a lot of little brown ants were needed to make a breakfast for a ten-inch lizard.

Grid twitched his tail over his back.

Not far from the anthill was a sunny slope where grasshoppers began to jump. Grid saw them with one eye. Then he turned so that he could watch them better, standing with his front legs almost straight and his hind ones braced to start him running. Next he bobbed up and down a few times, lifted his black and white tail, jerked it, and gave his head a funny shake. By that time he seemed to make up his mind. *Zipp!* he ran, straight toward the grasshoppers. When one of them jumped, Grid jumped too. His body was a foot above the ground when he caught that first big spotted grasshopper.

Even the alert Grid could not catch every jumping grasshopper. He watched closely and darted very quickly, but he often missed his prey. After chasing grasshoppers for about ten minutes, he had had enough of that exercise. So he lifted his tail and ran off, glancing this way and that. Perhaps he might find a grub, a cricket, or some crane flies that were resting on the ground.

Grid was looking for food so intently that he almost missed seeing a larger lizard that sat beside some brown rocks. Not until the big fellow made a dash for him, did Grid know that any such thing was near. In a moment he was flashing across the desert, tail up as usual. Guided by the banded tail ahead of him, the other lizard gave chase until he found that Grid was getting farther and farther away. Becoming tired of that sort of hunting, the larger lizard stopped. He found it much pleasanter to prowl under a creosote bush. Perhaps he might find a cicada sitting quietly on a low branch. He liked cicadas, or other insects, quite as well as lizard meat.

The startled Grid was tired too. Soon he stopped and crouched near a stone. There he found a spot where the sand was loose. Wiggling his head from side to side in the sand for a few moments and pushing with his long-toed feet, he was so nearly covered with sand that he seemed just a part of the ground. Another hungry lizard passed him, without knowing he was there. And Grid? He shut his eyes and lay there, glad of a chance to rest and be safe. It was very comforting to be able to turn himself into what seemed to be sand. Just now he was not waving that banded tail of his!

SPOT, THE LEOPARD LIZARD

The creature that gave Grid such a scare was Spot, the leopard lizard. Though only three inches longer than Grid, he was considerably heavier and had a much bigger head. His tail and back were light brown, with spots of darker brown and creamy white. Some of the spots on his tail ran together, forming irregular rings.

When he wanted to look about, Spot spread his hind legs close to the ground and lifted his big flattish head. As he did this, on pausing near the creosote bush, he saw a large black fly sitting on a pebble two feet away. Spot stuck out his tongue and started to crawl, going slowly and carefully. The fly buzzed away and he followed for a time, but gave up the chase when

Spot lifted his big head.

the fly sailed across an arroyo. Spot seemed not to like running or walking in the open desert but preferred to stay near bushes. Perhaps that was why he gave up so quickly when Grid ran away from the creosote bushes.

Spot acted as if he were the greediest lizard on the desert where Testudo, Grid, and he lived. He gobbled flies and beetles and cicadas every time he could catch them. He ate lizards of different kinds. He even ate very young leopard lizards, which were darker and more brightly colored than he was. Once, when he was only eleven inches long, Spot had swallowed a ten-inch gridiron-tailed lizard without biting it.

After missing both Grid, who escaped over the open desert, and the fly that went over the arroyo, Spot saw a cicada on one of the creosote twigs. It was too high to be reached from the ground, and leopard lizards are not good at climbing. What Spot did was to run a few feet and then jump. He sailed two feet into the air; and when he came down, the dark body of the cicada was sliding down his wrinkled throat.

As he wandered from bush to bush, Spot sometimes met his mate. In April she looked very much as he did. By late June or July she would be very different. Her sides would turn salmon-pink or salmon-red, and so would the under side of her tail. She might have bright red spots on the salmon-colored places. Not long after getting these bright colors, she would lay three or four eggs, each about half an inch long. Then she would go away and busy herself with eating. She did not see a slender five-inch baby hatch from each half-inch egg.

65

Why should either Father or Mother Spot stay round to help children who could catch food for themselves the very first time they ever felt hungry?

WHIP-TAIL

Though Whip-tail and Grid lived in the same desert, hunting under the same bushes, they never tried to become acquainted. Lizards, you see, are not sociable. They enjoy the companionship of their mates for a few days each spring, but live alone the rest of the year. They do not even recognize their own brothers and sisters. So you would not expect Whip-tail to make friends with lizards of other kinds, or with peaceful tortoises like Testudo.

Whip-tail and Grid, to be sure, often met without being afraid of each other and running away to hide. But both of them kept watch for greedy Spot, who would have liked to gobble either of them down whole.

Whip-tail was about two inches longer than Grid, and she had a very different shape. Her legs were not nearly so long as those of a gridiron lizard, and her head was narrow and pointed. The longest part of her body was her tail. This was more than twice the length of the rest of her body—head and all. No wonder it reminded people of a whip!

Usually, Whip-tail did not run quickly. She liked to prowl under creosote bushes, dragging herself along the ground and slinking from side to side as she stepped. The brown, gray, and bluish marks on her body made her look a good deal like the shadows on dry, fallen leaves. Her tail might be mistaken for a gray stick, unless sunshine gleamed on its bright, smooth scales.

Whip-tail's tail was the longest part of her body.

Still, Whip-tail could run. In times of danger she could move very rapidly indeed. Only a few days ago a coyote saw her and thought it would be pleasant to have such a pretty lizard for a morning meal. He was just ready to pounce and snap, when Whip-tail darted over the sand with her tail sticking up in the air and twitching as she went. After a while she paused, almost as if waiting for the coyote to catch up with her and start another race. She watched him until he came near; then she hurried away again. After she did that five or six times, the little wolf became discouraged and gave up the chase. Whip-tail rested before she crept under the nearest saltbush and hunted for beetles.

When busy in this way, Whip-tail used her slinking walk. She stuck her pointed blue-gray nose into every pile of leaves or sticks, and into almost every crack. When she found a beetle she caught it by thrusting out her sticky tongue. She captured ants, spiders, and even grasshoppers in the same way.

Often she paused and raised her head, as if to look and listen for danger. At times she seemed to know what might hurt her and what might not. She paid no attention to doves and sparrows, but she dodged under a thick bush every time a hawk appeared. She had run away from a coyote, but she did not seem really afraid of a big dog who trotted down the trail quite near her. She ran only a short distance and then forgot to be timid. She acted in the same manner when two brown burros, followed by a man in heavy boots, came along the trail on their way to get water from the spring in the oasis. If dog, burro, or man had chased her, she would have scampered farther off; but if they did not trouble her, why should she worry?

When June came, Whip-tail began to welcome the company of lizards of her own shiny-scaled kind. It was then she met her mate. He was at least an inch shorter than she, but he had the same pretty, glistening colors.

They played together among the bushes and stones, hunted insects under brushy mesquite trees, and wriggled between dry leaves that dropped from palms at the oasis. They seemed to have a happy time together—yet after a few days, Mr. Whip-tail went off by himself and Mrs. Whip-tail was quite content to return to her lone hunting under the creosote bushes.

One morning she was more restless than usual. She

nosed out spiders for a while but soon lost interest in them. Then she went off to a bank of soft sand and really began to work. She dug a hole with her front feet, laid her small eggs in it, covered them well with sand, and departed. Her babies, like those of Mrs. Grid and Mother Spot, needed no help from their parents when they hatched.

After leaving her nest full of eggs, Whip-tail felt like taking a rest. But first she must make her bed. On a slope near the palm trees, she found a place where the sand suited her. So, here, she began to dig with her front feet—a stroke with one foot and then with the other. Or, part of the time, she dug for quite a while with her right foot and then rested that while she used her left one. When the sand piled up in her way, she crawled into the hole; then she came out, pushing the sand with her paws. At last the hole was big enough. Whip-tail crept in and turned round. With her head pointed outward, she settled down to a day of safety and quiet. Didn't she deserve that much, after laying her year's supply of eggs?

CHAPTER VII

A WOLF-SPIDER AND RELATIVES

LYCOSA OF THE WHITE SANDS

LYCOSA was spending the day at home, which was just what she liked to do. The desert, outside, was bright and dry and hot in the daytime—not at all the kind of place which Lycosa enjoyed. Her home was cool, damp, and dark, and Lycosa was comfortable there.

Lycosa's home was a tunnel almost ten inches long. Its doorway was round and lined with silk, and it had no door to cover it. The lining went down about an inch and a half below ground. It kept the round doorway from crumbling when the sand at the surface became dry and loose. Below that lining of silk, the sand never became really dry, even though there was very little rain on the desert. For about six inches the tunnel went straight down, and then it turned into a sloping den. The firm, moist walls of the tunnel and slanting rooms at the bottom did not crumble. Lycosa did not need to line them with silk.

This is because she lived in a very special kind of desert, the White Sands of New Mexico. The white sands are not hard and gritty, like the common *quartz* sands. They are soft, with a creamy or even a pure white color, for they are grains of the mineral called *gypsum*. Gypsum is used to make plaster of Paris and crayons for writing on blackboards. Neither of those is very hard. This same material is used, too, in many other ways.

Where the White Sands are piled up in hills or ridges or spread out in flats, there once was a shallow lake. Even now, much water seeps down from the mountains at the edge of the desert. It seeps underground for miles and miles. Then it comes to the surface and evaporates, rising between the grains of white sand. Only the surface layer becomes dry. The seeping water keeps all the rest of the gypsum moist. This is why the walls of Lycosa's tunnel always are damp and firm except near the doorway.

Lycosa probably was pleased with her home, for she made it herself. She worked many nights, digging up grains of the gypsum and bringing them to her doorway. She piled some of them round her doorway and made it a little higher; but she threw the rest of the grains into her dooryard where the wind could blow them away. After she dug her room, or den, with a slanting floor at the bottom of the tunnel, she rested there during the sunny hours. She always ran down to it to hide when any animal came close to her open doorway.

Besides doing all that digging and carrying, Lycosa spun the silk that lined her entrance. The silk she made

71

Lycosa's home was near this Yucca in the white sands.

was much like that which a caterpillar spins. First it was a liquid, thicker than water, in silk glands inside her body. It did not harden into a thread until Lycosa squeezed it out through her *spinnerets*. A caterpillar has two silk glands that connect with a narrow, tube-shaped spinneret that opens through its lower lip. Lycosa's spinnerets were not close to her mouth. They were small, jointed affairs near the tip of her abdomen.

Though the hairs on Lycosa's body were gray, she was not old. She was much too young to be Mother Lycosa and lay eggs. She still was Miss Lycosa on the evening when four people saw her walking across the soft white sand.

These people knew that the word *lycosa* means *wolf*. They noticed that Lycosa walked round like a tiny lone wolf when she was hunting. They had met other wolf spiders who were hunting in woods and on hillsides far away from any desert. They wondered what Lycosa would find to eat. A black beetle, perhaps, for there were many of them living among the grass and yuccas that grew in hollows between the sand hills. Perhaps a young grasshopper, almost as light-colored as the sands themselves. Perhaps some other insect that was hiding under the dead leaves scattered near a tall yucca.

Lycosa did not care which insect she caught, so long as she did not have to go far for it. She looked among the first wisps of grass and hurried on to a little saltbush. There she just missed a fine grasshopper, who managed to jump out of the way even though he was rather sleepy. She soon found a dead fly, but that was

73

Lycosa came out to hunt at sunset.

too dry for her to eat. At last she came to a lazy, stiff beetle and pounced upon it very swiftly. She reached for a soft place in the beetle's body, between joints, and bit it there with her strong jaws. Then she picked it up and with high, quick steps carried it back to her home. She did not stop to eat her supper out of doors. Why should she, when she had a good safe room where other hunters could not find her?

The four visitors did not bother Lycosa. They stood still and watched her while she hurried across the sand in the bright moonlight. When she came to her door, one of them called, "Good luck, Lycosa!" Then they walked away and climbed the nearest sand hill. Soon they would reach their own homes, which were tents, and cook their own supper (a very big one!) on a gasoline stove.

TA-RAN-TU-LA

Old Ta was waiting on the mountain slope that night, much as she had waited other summer nights for nearly twenty years. Behind her was her home, where she had dug a doorway leading to a hollow under a flat stone. Below her the desert sands spread out at the foot of the mountain. There were shadows among the near rocks while the distant desert lay open to the moonlight. The sands of this desert were not white even when the sun shone on them. Their color was grayish brown. Ta dwelt at the edge of a desert miles away from her relative of the White Sands.

The desert was pleasant in the moonlight, but Ta saw neither the rocks close to her nor the sands far away. There was nothing really wrong with her eight glistening eyes. They were just as good as they ever had been—and not a bit better. In the daytime she could sense the difference between the dark corner of her hole and the bright sunlight outside, though she could not see quiet objects either by day or night.

Her name, Ta-ran-tu-la, is a musical word, but Ta was not singing as she waited in front of her hole that night. Like other spiders, she had no voice, and so could not sing or shout even when she felt happy.

Although she was voiceless and practically blind, you need not feel sorry for Ta. She was content. She was not restless. Even when she was hunting, she did it in a patient way. Usually she merely stayed near her home until a cricket or cockroach or other insect

Ta's mate came to visit her in the fall.

wandered near enough to touch her. Then she captured her prey by leaning back on her hind legs and hitting and holding it with her front legs. As soon as she had a good hold, she could nip the insect with her clawlike mouth parts from the tips of which she squeezed out a little poison. Ta could do all this very quickly indeed, without thinking just what she was doing.

Ta did not have a banquet of this sort every evening. Sometimes she waited four or five nights, or even a week or two, without catching anything at all. She did not starve or really suffer where there was such a wait between meals, and she fasted for a longer period each winter. But she had a good appetite and enjoyed feasting as often as she had any food.

It was not only at night that Ta came out of her hole. She often went outdoors during the day, too. That was when she brought her big cocoon, or egg sac, where it could be warmed by the sunshine. While it was sunning, she always stayed near to guard it. If anything came near enough to disturb her, Ta quickly took her egg sac back into her tunnel where it would be safe. Ta had more than six hundred eggs in that sac of spider silk, and she was not going to run any risk of losing them!

During most of each year, Ta lived alone. After her eggs hatched, the baby spiders stayed in the cocoon until they were ready to molt for the first time. (While they were young and growing rapidly they molted, or shed their skins, rather often. When they were older, they did this only once a year.) That usually was in August. So she was not really "alone" when there were hundreds of young spiders in her home—even though they were shut up inside the silken sac.

Then in September or October Mr. Ta came to visit her. So she had company for a while each fall, too.

If you had met big Ta one June day while she was sunning her eggs, you would have known that she was a spider. Her body was divided into two parts as was that of Lycosa. Her head and thorax were joined together to make one part, and her abdomen formed the second part. She had eight legs, too, and eight is the proper number of legs for a spider.

Would you have been afraid of Ta, if you had seen her? Perhaps. Some people fear even small spiders, and certainly old Ta was not small. She measured more than two inches and a half from the front of her head to the tip of her abdomen. Yet she would not have hurt you if you had stopped and watched her; and you would have found her interesting.

You might even have liked Ta, for people who know most about tarantulas really do like them. There is Dr. W. J. Baerg, for example, who calls them "charming creatures." You may like to read an article of his called, "Tarantulas as Pets."[5]

[5]*Nature Magazine*, March, 1927, pages 173-176.

SOL PUGID

Yes, you can tell that a tarantula is only a big hairy spider, just by looking at it. But *what* would you have thought about queer Sol Pugid if you had lifted the stone she was hiding under?

If she had rushed toward your hand, snapping her strong, sharp pincers open and shut, you would have dodged out of her way without stopping to ask her name. And no one could blame you for being startled, for she could act as if she were very fierce indeed.

However, you need not have stayed frightened. At least, people who have let solpugids bite them say that the pincers do not nip very hard. These mouth parts can keep hold of insects they catch, but people need not worry about them.

Sol Pugid

If you meet a real creature of this kind, or look at a picture of one, you may think for a minute that it is an insect of some strange sort. Its body is divided into three distinct parts—head, thorax, and abdomen. It resembles an insect in this respect. But how many legs has it? Five pairs? Well, who ever heard of a ten-footed insect? An insect, whether it is a hornet or a beetle or a grasshopper or a dragonfly, or what not, has six legs only.

We would better tell you something about that first pair of long jointed things that look like legs. They are not legs really. They are pedipalps (*ped* means *foot*, and *palp* means *feeler*); and although a solpugid sometimes uses them in walking, it also uses them to feel with.

Since the pedipalps are not true legs, you can see that Sol has only four pairs of true legs. So, after all, she is eight-legged, like a spider.

Indeed, solpugids are much more closely related to spiders than they are to insects. They resemble scorpions, too, in many ways. People in the Southwest commonly call these creatures "wind scorpions" because they run so very swiftly.

And when people speak of wind scorpions, they usually chuckle. Why? Well, if you had seen Sol snapping her pincers, you would probably have laughed too, after you found that you need not be frightened. There was something very comical about her—even when she was trying to be fierce!

CHAPTER VIII

THREE LARGE LIZARDS

CHUCK, WHO LIKED ROCKS

CHUCK WALLA sat on a ledge of granite and looked. Just how far he could see with his eyes, we do not know. If you should sit on that high ledge, you could see the side of a dry, brown mountain range with valleys whose floors are covered with sand. Still farther away

A Rocky Scene near Chuck's Home

81

is a sloping desert. If the air were very clear, you could see the shapes of palm trees growing near some desert springs on an oasis.

There are no springs of bubbling water where Chuck lives. The rocks and sand are dry. Still, there are many green plants near his home. That very morning, Chuck had hidden under a juniper tree when a big hawk had tried to catch him. From the juniper he went to a clump of yuccas.

Near Chuck's ledge there are cactus plants of several kinds. One of them has broad, flat joints that are brownish green and look like velvet because they are covered with tufts of short hairs. This cactus is not so soft as it looks, however, for the hairs are very prickly. "Beaver-tail cactus," people call it when they spend their vacations in Chuck's neighborhood. This is a good name

Beaver-tail Cactus

for it, because its joints remind one of the broad, flat tail of a beaver.

What kind of a creature is Chuck himself? He is a lizard whose full name you may write "chuckwalla" or "chuckawalla," as you prefer. From his nose to the blunt tip of his tail, he is about sixteen inches long. His head, neck, and legs are brownish black; his body is brown with dark brown and black spots; his tail is pale orange with dull black bands.

Do you think, because you know Chuck's colors, that you know those of all his close relatives? Some of Chuck's own brothers have backs that are yellow instead of brown, with red spots in place of black. One of his cousins has a dark back with yellow spots, yellow scales on his legs, and a tail that is dull yellow with bands of brown. You can't tell whether a lizard is a chuckwalla or not just by looking at his colors! You need to notice the shape of its queer, thick body.

Chuck is a cautious creature. He has to be careful. His flesh is very good to eat. Foxes, coyotes, hawks, owls, and even some people like the taste of chuckwalla meat. If any of them should catch Chuck, he could hit with his strong, thick tail. But would that hurt a coyote or scare away a hungry hawk?

So, while Chuck lay in the bright sunshine, he kept a very careful watch. Something moved. Chuck lifted his head and eyed it closely. It was only a peaceful jack rabbit. Jack rabbits, of course, never eat lizards, so there was no reason why Chuck should not settle down to his sunning. A falling rock caused him to lift his head again; but the rock had been knocked loose by a burro, who was just as harmless as the jack rabbit. Chuck's eyes almost closed—and then a hawk soared through the air, its shadow crossing Chuck's open ledges. At once the big lizard dodged into a crack. He did not come out for half an hour after the hawk disappeared.

Had a coyote, not a hawk, startled Chuck he would have gone into that very same crack. He would have puffed out his body with big gulps of air until he was twice his usual size. Then let something try to pull him out through that narrow crack between the great rocks!

When Chuck returned to the sunshine on his ledge, he found a straw-colored chuckwalla sitting in his favorite place. Chuck shook his head and hissed, but the stranger did not go away. Chuck hissed and stamped his feet; then he ran at the other lizard, shoving, swinging his tail, and biting. Before long the newcomer ran from the ledge as fast as he could, and scrambled up a stone of his own. He found himself quite comfortable there, for after all he was not very much hurt by any of Chuck's bumps and bites.

As the morning turned into afternoon, the rock in Chuck's ledge became hotter and hotter. A bird who hopped onto it fluttered away at once, while a man who came by and touched it said *"Ouch!"* and withdrew his hand. But Chuck seemed to find it very pleasant. Such heat made him far keener and quicker that he ever was on cool mornings.

Later in the afternoon, Chuck felt hungry. He left the ledge and clambered over rocks to a place where

Chuck sat on a granite ledge.

some desert tea (or Mormon tea) was growing. This plant looks like the scouring rushes (or "horsetails") which you may have found growing in moist places. Most of the stems were tough, but Chuck found a few fairly tender tips and ate them. Next he came to some burr ragweeds, or burro weeds. Many people dislike these plants, because their bright yellow pollen makes them sneeze and causes them to have "hay fever." The pollen never bothered Chuck, however. When he found two fresh clumps of burro weed, he made a good meal of them. Still he had room for leaves from a creosote bush. These strong-scented leaves often were a favorite part of Chuck's menu. He did not chew his food much but swallowed it almost as soon as he bit it off the plants, so perhaps he did not take time really to taste all the strange flavors in the tender blossoms and leaves he ate. He seemed to like almost any flower or leaf he found, if it was not too dry and hard.

When his supper was eaten, Chuck started home. He walked with jerky movements and stuck out his tongue every few steps. He also stopped to look and listen. The moment he saw a coyote, *whish!*—Chuck was in a deep crack, getting bigger and bigger every moment. And there he stayed all night, though the coyote soon tired of pawing at a lizard that simply could *not* be pulled out.

GILA

Gila (whose name is pronounced *He-la*) lived a long way from Chuck, though her home, too, was in a mountain. What you might see, by looking over *her* valley, are a lot of spiny, flat-jointed cacti called prickly pears and some very tall ones named giant cacti, or sahuaros. You could also see a creek, for melting snow on high peaks sends water down to the place where Gila lived.

Gila was bigger than Chuck. Her body was a foot and a half long and so thick it seemed almost round. Gila's tail was plump and round, too, with fat stored away under its skin. In the winter, when Gila slept under a rock, she lived for weeks without eating. All she had to do was to use the fat in her tail. There was enough of it to keep her from starving.

Gila climbed up on a rock.

In the summer, however, Gila did a great deal of feasting. Would you like to know what she ate one evening before she climbed up on a rock? First she found some young ground squirrels, which she swallowed before they knew what was happening. Then she came to a nest of soft-shelled eggs laid by some other lizard. With her stubby front feet she dug for them one at a time, swallowing each one as soon as she pawed it out. By that time she was so nearly satisfied that she ate only a few of the crickets that were lurking among the rocks near her creek.

She was no longer hungry enough even to hunt for those good-tasting crickets, but she was thirsty. She knew her way to the creek, so she went there for a good long drink. She even took a bath by going into shallow water which washed the dust from her rough, knobby skin. That was one reason why her orange spots seemed so very bright and her dark spots so black.

Another reason was that she had shed her old, rather dingy skin not long ago and now had a fresh new suit.

After her supper and her drink and her bath, Gila climbed a rock and stayed there for some time. She felt comfortable and lazy and had nothing else to do that evening.

One late afternoon not long after that, however, she had such an important errand that she did not linger on her rock. Instead, she pulled her big body over the edge and waddled down toward the creek. Its bank was coarse gravel in which it would not be easy for her to dig. So she did not stop before coming to sand that was fine and loose. Though damp, it still was quite warm from the heat of the afternoon sun.

This warm sand was just what Gila wanted. Kicking her front feet awkwardly, she dug a hole about four inches deep. In that hole she laid nine eggs that had soft, though tough, shells. Each egg was two and one-half inches long. She covered these eggs by scraping the hole full of sand, and then she went away. There was nothing more she could do for them. The sun would keep the eggs warm. In a month nine little lizards would hatch from them, each baby four inches long and shaped like its clumsy mother.

Like most reptiles that live on land, Gila could not do very much when her body became too chilly. But, like some snakes in the desert, she did not like to get too hot, either. One noon, she was resting in the shade of a big dead bush when suddenly the wind blew her shelter away. Gila was caught in the sunshine at noon on a summer day. In a few minutes she felt very uncomfortable. She began to hiss and snap, making froth in her mouth. She seemed to be almost crazy before she twisted and jerked her way into the shadow of a rock. That place in the shade seemed very pleasant to her, and in a little while she went happily to sleep. After her frantic time in the sunshine, she was tired.

When Gila was startled she did not escape to a crack and hide as Chuck did. She stayed where she was and fought for her safety. One day she became very, very angry. She had reason to be furious, for two men found her and poked her with sticks. Gila paid no attention to them at first, so the men poked her harder and harder. Then she began to snap her jaws, moving her head much more quickly than the men were able to move their sticks. It was surprising to see Gila, usually so slow, now when she was really excited. Once she jumped up, whirled rapidly round, and bit a stick very close to the bare hand of one of the men. Getting a hold on the stick she chewed at it, grinding her jaws together fiercely. Again a frothy stuff showed between her hard lips.

The men did not touch that froth, for they knew it was a kind of poison made by glands under Gila's chin. It flowed out of those glands and up grooves in Gila's strong, short teeth. If she had been biting the flesh of some creature that was bothering her, Gila would have got some of that poison into the wound her teeth made. There would have been enough to kill a small animal and enough to make a man very sick.

This is why the men kept their hands out of Gila's reach. They watched her savagely chew the stick. While she was doing this one of the men wrote something in a small brown notebook. The other made a drawing on a leaf in his sketchbook. After they had finished, they stood a few minutes looking down at Gila.

"Let's not harm her," said the artist. "I needed a picture of an angry Gila Monster, or I should not have disturbed her."

"I don't blame her for getting violent," remarked the writer. "She would not have tried to attack us if we had not poked her with those sticks. She was only defending herself, and she had a right to do that."

So the two men walked away. After a time Gila became calm enough to go slowly down to the creek and take a soothing drink of water.

CROTA

Crota, the collared lizard, sunned himself beside a red stone. Long ago—long *ages* ago—that stone was part of a big tree. It grew in the forest when the Painted Desert was a swampy forest through which sluggish rivers flowed. In fact, it was one of the very trees killed by a forest fire started by lightning during a thunderstorm.

Crota sunned himself beside a red stone.

91

Of course Crota did not know what fire was. Neither did he know anything about different kinds of trees. The only one he had ever seen was a little twisted cottonwood that grew near a petrified log. It was smaller than just one branch of the pinelike trees that lived in that same country ages and ages ago.

That lizard could not even fully realize what an elegant coat of skin he was wearing, but he acted as if he knew all about it. He seemed proud of his rich green suit with its two black collars on his neck. He seemed proud of the pale yellow spots on his back and the orange specks on his eyes. He acted as if he liked all the gay colors that decorated his twelve inches of head, body, and tail.

If Crota really felt that way, it was because he was looking for a mate. After strutting about for three or four days, he found her. She was slaty gray with shadings of green and almost no orange spots. She also seemed delighted with Crota's bright colors when he marched up and down to show them to her. She watched closely when he puffed out his throat and displayed its dark orange hues.

They lived together for a few days; then Mrs. Crota went away. Crota stayed among his own petrified logs, where he caught little lizards and grasshoppers. He also lunched on crickets and a few baby snakes—a few, because there were not many for him to catch. Beetles, spiders, and flowers also served for part of his meals. Such food was small for a foot-long lizard, and Crota

kept himself busy much of the time, just finding enough
to eat.

Still, he did not hunt all day. On cool mornings,
he hid in cracks between chunks of petrified wood. At
such times his skin did not have its bright blue-green
color; it was dark, dull greenish gray. But when the air
grew hot Crota started out to hunt, and his skin began
to turn green again. By ten o'clock he was almost as
bright as he could be, and quick enough to catch his
swiftest prey.

Crota was on the watch for hawks and foxes, for
he wished to keep out of their way. He also felt wary of
people. Many of them came to see the broken trunks
of petrified trees lying on the ground, and the places
they visited happened to be some of Crota's best hunting
grounds. So, often he dodged under bushes or slipped
behind chunks of logs to escape being seen. Every now
and then, too, he would be alarmed enough to run from
the top of a big trunk, where he liked to lie and sun
himself during the hottest part of the day.

Sometimes children would chase Crota—not to
hurt him but just to see him run. He did have a queer
manner of getting away from them. He would start out
on all four legs, going very fast indeed. In a moment
he would be on his hind legs, going even faster. If
something was in the way, he jumped over it. Many
times he leaped over logs as much as two feet high. No
one ever caught him, or even got very close to him; but
grown people, as well as children, thought it great fun
to see Crota sail over the long, red trunks.

While Crota was sunning himself, hunting for food, and racing here and there, something was happening to Mother Crota. Her skin was changing its colors. Her back became less dull and her sides turned a brick red. Red spots appeared on her legs and tail. Indeed, she was almost as bright, if not quite so pretty, as Father Crota had been weeks before when she first met him.

When the red began to show on her legs, Mother Crota spent a great deal of her time poking about under stones. At last she found a place that seemed to please her. She turned round two or three times and dug a wide, shallow hole. In it she laid twenty eggs, each two-thirds of an inch long. Then she scraped sand over them and trotted away to eat crickets. Her babies, like those of other lizards, would take care of themselves when they hatched.

A few weeks later, Father Crota was hunting near that very same stone. He saw something moving beneath its edge. It was not a grasshopper or cricket. No, it was a baby collared lizard, the first of the twenty to hatch. Crota watched it for a moment and then went on his way. How could he know that tiny lizard was one of his own children?

CHAPTER IX

CACTUS WRENS

WHICH wren do you know best—the house wren? That is the pert little chap who can pass through a round hole as small as a twenty-five-cent piece without squeezing his feathers. He sings his tinkly sort of burble as if he were in a hurry; but he has plenty of time to repeat it again and again.

Or is it the winter wren whose voice you like so well that you sometimes wait in the woods to hear his happy melody? He stays out of sight most of the time; but if you should happen to catch a glimpse of him you might notice that he is even smaller than the house wren.

If you have known these or his other small relatives, you will not say, "Why, there is a wren!" the first time you see a cactus wren. For this desert dweller is different in many ways. His body is too big and his tail is too long and his breast is too spotted to remind you of a wren at all.

Perhaps you will say (many people do), "Wasn't that a brown thrasher that flew away from the cholla just then?" Of course, when you get a really good look

*The people of Arizona like the cactus wren well enough
to call it their "state bird."*

at him, you can see that you have made a mistake. The white stripe over each eye and the black bars on his tail, as well as other markings, show that he is not a brown thrasher either. Besides, although he is giant-sized for a wren, he is not so large as a brown thrasher.

It is quite likely that you will hear him before you see him, for he often calls with a loud clattering voice. Some people, visiting the desert, wonder what can be making that racket, and they walk among the cactus clumps to find out. It is not so easy to locate him as it might seem; because, as the wren turns his head, his voice sounds as if it comes from different directions. So the searchers go this way and that and, as likely as not, do not find the noisy bird at all. And after a while, when the bird is in the right mood, he will give the desert a real song—a full-throated alto tune, joyous to hear.

Is there anything else strange about these rollicking wrens? Yes, their nests. People who have tried to describe cactus wrens' nests have written that they are "purse-shaped," "retort-shaped," "pocket-shaped," "flask-shaped," and "gourd-shaped." Now, do you know how they look? About fifteen years ago a man named William Dawson made fun of the people who called these nests "purse-shaped," and the like. He said that cactus wrens build nests shaped like *footballs!* We might add that they are often as large as watermelons.

In the chapter about Pep we met some cactus wrens that made their nest in a tangle of desert mistletoe on a mesquite tree. If you travel through the desert regions of the Southwest, you may find their nests in many other places. Perhaps you will see one placed in a big clump of prickly pears or resting in the branches of a cat's-claw bush or held in the arm of a sahuaro or built among the sharp bayonet-like leaves of a big yucca. But most often you will find one in the spiniest thing in the desert—the cholla cactus.

A Cholla is a very spiny cactus. This is a small one.
A larger one is pictured in the next chapter.

That is where Yodeler and his mate had their nest. Yodeler really enjoyed building a nest as much as Pep did, but he did not insist on making nearly all of it. He was quite willing to have his mate bring as many twigs and plant stems as she wished and place them just where she thought they should go. Indeed, she made most of the nest in which later she was to put her eggs. Soon after that one was done, Yodeler went off by himself and built a few other nests in chollas not far away. He used one of these for a bedroom at night.

While Mr. and Mrs. Yodeler were gathering stuff for their most important nest (the one for the eggs), they brought thorny sticks and stiff strawy grass stems. They picked strong slender stems with little clusters of flowers and stems with downy white leaves that looked woolly.

These sticks and stems they piled in a rough mass as big as a watermelon lying on its side. This did not have an opening on top as Pep's nest did, or as the nests of most birds do. It opened at one end.

Inside the rough framework Mrs. Yodeler put a padded wall and floor and ceiling of shredded bark, dried flowers, and grass. For an inner lining she used still softer materials, such as spider silk and as many feathers as she could find. The doorway from this domed nest opened into a narrow tunnel that led out among the prickly cholla joints.

You could not reach your hand into a nest of this sort without getting badly scratched and stabbed, but the two Yodelers passed in and out without even tearing their feathers or hurting their feet.

After Mrs. Yodeler had laid her five eggs, one each day, she spent most of her time for about a fortnight sitting on them, though she slipped out through the hallway tunnel and flew off for food when she needed it.

Two Young Cactus Wrens

Her pretty eggs had pale buffy-salmon shells sprinkled with cinnamon-brown spots. Not long after the eggs hatched the five naked baby wrens opened their mouths all at once, like a singing quintet—only they were not singing. They were begging for food.

Father Yodeler helped his mate hunt for desert insects to feed the youngsters. It took a great deal of insect meat to keep those little birds properly supplied, for each baby ate much more than its father or mother. The parent wrens were very busy until the day came when the young Yodelers could creep out through the tunnel at the end of their nest and face the thorny desert world.

By this time the youngsters had good coats of dappled feathers, though their breasts were not so thickly spotted as those of their parents and their tails were not yet so long. They lacked the experience that the old birds had with cactus spines; and they had to practice a bit before they learned how to perch on a prickly cholla stem without hurting their feet. These youngsters had to get used to many new things.

It took some practicing, too, before they could catch all the insects they needed to eat. So, even after they could fly a little, they spent several days begging their parents for food. They still were rather greedy, but Father and Mother Yodeler did not let the young wrens get too hungry. The old birds brought them weevils and other beetles, grasshoppers, crickets, and even wasps, until the young Yodelers were able to do their own hunting.

As you may know, young birds of most kinds never go back to their home nest after they are old enough to leave it. The young Yodelers, too, were happy enough away from their nest during the day. It had become really too crowded for them. Although the outside was as big as a watermelon, the walls had so many sticks and stems and so much stuffing that the rapidly growing youngsters had been crammed a bit too much during their last hours there. They did not feel homesick. The desert had been very roomy and pleasant during the bright, warm, sunshiny day.

But evening drew near and something happened to their feelings as the desert changed. The air was chilly and they wanted shelter. There were bushes within sight, but their leaves were not big enough to offer any protection. They could perch on cholla joints, but it was cold there, too. Besides, if they moved a bit carelessly during the night those spines might jab them.

Restlessly the young Yodelers took short flights and hopped here and there. Then suddenly they found the best of bedrooms—those nests Yodeler had made while they were inside their egg shells! These nests did not have such warm feathery linings as their first home had had, but that was all right. The young birds had their own fluffy feathers. They were not restless any more. They were contented and ready to spend a quiet night. They did not know that good old Dad Yodeler had built those nests just because he enjoyed doing it. It was enough for them to find these shelters, so cosy and homelike for the night.

CHAPTER X

JACK WITH THREE BLACK TIPS

THE sun was making the desert warm as Jack hopped over the sand. He had spent the night under a silver-colored shrubby plant with yellow daisy-like flowers. Jack did not know that human beings call this plant "brittle bush" because they can break it easily. He had no name for it, but he knew that brittle bush gave good shelter at night and in the brightest part of the day. Yet when morning came he always was ready to leave it and go out for his breakfast.

As he hopped, Jack passed many sahuaros. A sahuaro is a giant cactus with a thick, tall trunk. Ridges run up and down the trunk, and on each ridge there are bunches of long curved spines. Jack could see these sharp spines, and he never was careless or foolish enough to prick his tender skin on them.

One sahuaro that Jack passed had very large branches. Though Jack did not know it, they meant that the cactus was very old. At least two hundred years had passed since it first began to grow in the dry, sandy soil.

The Big Sahuaro near Jack's Home

They were not easy years, either. Scars showed where the cactus had been injured, and rings on its branches told of dry years when water was scarcer than usual. The big cactus got its share, even then but some of its neighbors were not so lucky. Jack hopped near one whose branches had wilted and had never been able to reach up again. Instead, they drooped and twisted like the arms on a huge scarecrow!

While Jack stopped to nibble some green leaves, a bird flew up to a round hole in the trunk of the big sahuaro. It stopped for a moment and then went in. Soon it came out of the hole again and flew away over the desert.

This busy bird was Sagu, a Gila woodpecker. The hole was the door to the home that he and Aro, his mate, had dug in the trunk of the giant cactus. With their strong, sharp beaks they had dug away at the tough fibers and soft pith. Soon sap began to drip. It splattered Sagu's black and white back, stuck to the gray-brown feathers on his breast, and dulled the red spot on his head. Aro had no red spot to be dulled, but her feathers were just as messy as those of her brighter colored mate.

Though the sap made the woodpeckers sticky, it also helped them build their home. When the digging was finished, the sap dried and lined the cavity with a layer as hard as wood. It made a good wall for the room in which Aro laid four white eggs. The babies that hatched from those eggs were hungry from day-light till dark.

Sagu was bringing food for their babies when he flew up to the hole. As he went back for more, he sang

Sagu, the Gila Woodpecker

a little song that went *"hint, hint!"* Mother Aro could not answer him, because her beak held a big beetle that she was going to feed to the hungriest baby.

While the woodpeckers worked, Jack hopped to a bush just beyond the giant cactus. Looking up, he could see a long-tailed bird perched at the tip of another sahuaro. Jack just wiggled his ears and began eating. No mere sparrow hawk could hurt a hare that weighed almost six pounds!

A moment later, another bird flew close. This was a big hawk with a brick-red tail, and Jack leaped high in the air as his long legs took him away in a hurry. Four jumps brought him to a big cholla, whose spines were so sharp that no hawk would dare to fly down among them. Even Jack hopped very carefully to keep from the prickly joints that had fallen to the ground.

Almost two years had passed since Jack first saw that big branched cholla. Then he was a tiny baby, only a few hours old. His fur was brown, with black and yellow hairs; his ears were short and almost round; his legs were so short that it seemed as if they never could become the legs of a full-grown jack rabbit. But even then Jack's teeth were cut and his eyes were wide open. His mother tucked him away in a nest of grass under this very same cholla. A few minutes later she brought Jack's sister and put her into the nest, too.

For a while the little hares snuggled down; then they began to play. They could walk and even hop a little, but they kept close to the ground and moved slowly. During the next three days, however, they really

Jack

began to jump. They also played a digging game. Both Jack and his sister spent a lot of time digging in some soft dirt near their nest. That was very, very strange. Neither their father nor their mother dug, and would not go into a hole even if chased by a fox.

When Jack was ten days old, his ears and legs began to lengthen. Soon his ears were as long as his furry head, while his legs had grown big and awkward. In three more weeks, he could pull the ends of his ears into his mouth and wash them. His sister could wash her ears too. Both could take long jumps with legs that were now strong.

Though they grew so fast, the young hares did not forget their mother; and luckily she did not forget them. Every night she came to feed them milk, the only kind of food they wanted. The twins were two weeks old before they even sniffed at green leaves. Then they touched them with their red tongues, nibbled a few bits from the edges, and went back to their digging and other play. Why eat leaves when milk tasted so much better?

For a while Mother Blacktail did not object, but at last she decided that her children should begin to look out for themselves. Though she still came to see them every night, she did not stay so long and she gave them less milk to drink. First the twins felt hungry; then they ate leaves and bits of grass that grew near the big cactus. In time they learned to like almost any leaves except the strong-tasting ones that grew on the creosote bushes. After that they did not seem to worry when Mother Blacktail stopped making her evening visits.

Now that they were old enough to be alone, Jack and his sister forgot about digging and spent more time in playing other games. They liked to chase each other among the bushes and cactus plants. They liked to jump over each other, to leap across little arroyos, and to play zigzag games on the sand. All this exercise helped to make them swift and strong. Soon the young hares were ready to take care of themselves in the big desert world.

One evening Jack's sister played a few minutes; then she hopped away. For a while Jack could watch her among the bushes, but soon she was out of sight. Jack did not know where she was going, and he did not follow to find out.

His sister might go away if she wished, but Jack was happy to stay where he was. He might travel a mile or so in one direction or another, but in a day or two he would be back near the place where Mother Blacktail first brought him. Even when a coyote chased him, Jack went in a big circle that left the small wolf behind and took him back to a clump of mesquite in sight of the big sahuaro cactus.

The creature that startled Jack most often was Kit, the little desert fox. He had a burrow in the ground under an old creosote bush, not far from Jack's cholla.

Kit slept in his burrow during the day. After sunset he came out to hunt insects, ground squirrels, and even the quails that sometimes made Pep angry by eating mistletoe berries. He never tried to catch Jack, but he often crept close to bushes where he was resting or eating. Once Kit barked right behind Jack's ears. That

Kit, the desert fox, hunts at night.

time the big hare jumped more than four feet into the air and dashed away with great leaps that carried him almost a mile in two minutes. Even when Jack was not in a hurry, his legs often made jumps of eight or ten feet, and that night he stretched those jumps to about fifteen feet. After that scare, two hours passed before he felt brave enough to come back and finish his supper of leaves.

By the time Jack could be as speedy as he was that night, he was, of course, fully grown. His heavy body was covered with soft fur that was yellowish brown mixed with cinnamon and black. His under parts were white, but his tail was black on top. The tips of his very large ears were black, too. His three black parts were rather showy in the daytime. He was one of those hares that are commonly spoken of as "black-tailed jack rabbits."

Most of Jack's frights had the same sort of happy ending. Whether he jumped away from a barking desert fox or dashed under a big cholla cactus to escape a red-tailed hawk, after a while he felt quite calm again—calm and hungry.

The Big Cholla

His hunger often led him to some scraggly old mesquite tree with its lowest branches trailing near the ground. There he stooped and feasted on the leaves he liked so well. And as he ate he worked his jaws so fast that they made a low, purring sound.

Perhaps the black-tailed jack rabbit you see, when you visit the desert, will be munching mesquite leaves like that. Before you get very close to him, he will be leaping across the sands; and as he goes you will get a glimpse of his three black tips.

CHAPTER XI

RACERS AND RATTLERS

RED RACER

RED RACER lay on the sand near a paloverde tree.[6] The paloverde tree had a green trunk, large green branches, and small green twigs. Most of the year it had no leaves, for they dropped a few days after they grew. When the tree was in blossom, thousands of pretty yellow flowers covered the green branches. Bees came buzzing among them to get pollen and sweet nectar.

It made no difference to Red Racer whether the tree had blossoms or leaves or bare branches. He was glad just to let the warm sun shine on his red-brown body, coiled beside a fallen branch. Now and then he lifted his head. It also was brown, with buff and pink shadings. Behind it were five dark brown bands that covered the top of Red Racer's neck. When he twisted his body a little, he showed that his under surface was a beautiful, glossy pink.

---

[6]*Palo* means *stick*, and *verde* means *green;* so a paloverde tree might be called a "green-stick tree."

A Paloverde tree under which Red Racer often rested.

As Red Racer grew warm, he uncoiled his long, slim body. Quietly he started to crawl. He did not squirm like some snakes; his body seemed to ripple, sending him in a straight line across the sand. That morning he glided slowly, pausing to poke his nose into brush piles and to look under prickly pears.

At a second paloverde tree he stopped, lifted his head, and began to climb. He did not wind himself *round* the trunk, but slipped straight up, moving his under scales against rough places on the bark. Do you think it would be hard to do this without any arms and legs with which to cling? It was not difficult for Red Racer. He climbed swiftly and easily.

115

Why did he go into the tree? Because he was hungry, and he often had good luck hunting in paloverdes. The lizards that are called *swifts* visited these branches to catch insects, and Red Racer thought they were good to eat. He also liked eggs and young birds. Perhaps he could find a hearty, varied breakfast if he glided through that paloverde!

This time, however, he was disappointed. He saw two spotted swifts, but they both dodged out of the way before he was near enough to reach them. He hoped, for a moment, that he could catch two young doves, but they were old enough to use their wings and so escaped him. There was only one nest in the tree and that was empty—not even an egg to eat. After slipping from branch to branch and making a thorough search, Red Racer went back to the ground as hungry as ever.

As he left the shelter of the tree and glided along the bare ground, a hawk swooped down from overhead. Red Racer saw her shadow moving—*zipp!* he flashed across the sand and hid under a big branching cholla. Not even the tip of his tail showed by the time the hawk was close enough to strike.

Under a creosote bush, later in the day, Red Racer met one of his own sons. The youngster was only about twelve inches long, a very very slender little snake. His scales were dark brownish gray, but they had the same satiny gloss that went with Red Racer's brighter colors. By the time he became full grown, his scales, like those of his father, would be rather large—making one think of the braids in a braided whip. Many people, for this reason, call a racer a "coach-whip snake."

Red Racer

By the time Red Racer caught his first swift, the sun was high and the day was very hot. As he crossed a bare acre of sand, the heat went right through his scales and made him hurry to the nearest shady place. He found a little shade under a clump of brittle brush, plants with silvery-gray leaves and yellow flowers. But their branches did not spread close to the ground and Red Racer could not manage to get all of his tail out of the sunshine. Next he tried a Mormon-tea shrub. This had a lot of branches but its leaves were only small scales; and it did not quite suit him, either. So he made a third attempt and crawled under a big burr ragweed where he remained for some time.

Later, however, he made his way to a paloverde tree under which there was a mass of dead branches on the ground. This was best of all, for he was really sheltered from the hot sun. He also was in a place where lizards often took refuge from swooping hawks. All he needed to do, now, was to keep awake and wait for his food to come to him. By noon, Red Racer even ceased trying to keep awake, for he had already caught all he wanted to eat. Why not take a nap in that comfortable, shady bed?

ATROX, THE DIAMOND RATTLER

Atrox lived in a rocky canyon, less than a mile from Red Racer's home. In the canyon were mesquite trees and large cat's-claw shrubs. The mesquite thorns were straight, while those of the cat's-claw were curved. Prospectors, who hunted in that canyon, called them "tear-blanket" and "wait-a-while."

It was not under the trees that Atrox lived. His home was a crack between two rocks, half hidden by brittle brush. Near it was a giant cactus whose branches twisted and turned downward, instead of pointing toward the sky. They grew that way because of a terrible drought, when water was so very scarce that all the giant cacti shrank and many of them wilted.

The crack where Atrox lived was in the north-facing side of the canyon, where the sun never made things so warm as it made the rocks facing southward. Still, there were times when it was too hot for comfort. In the summer, Atrox spent the middle of the day in his crack and came out to look for food in the evening or late afternoon. Had he been kept in a hot sunny place at midday, he would have suffered and perhaps even died.

Late afternoon was really pleasant. The sunshine

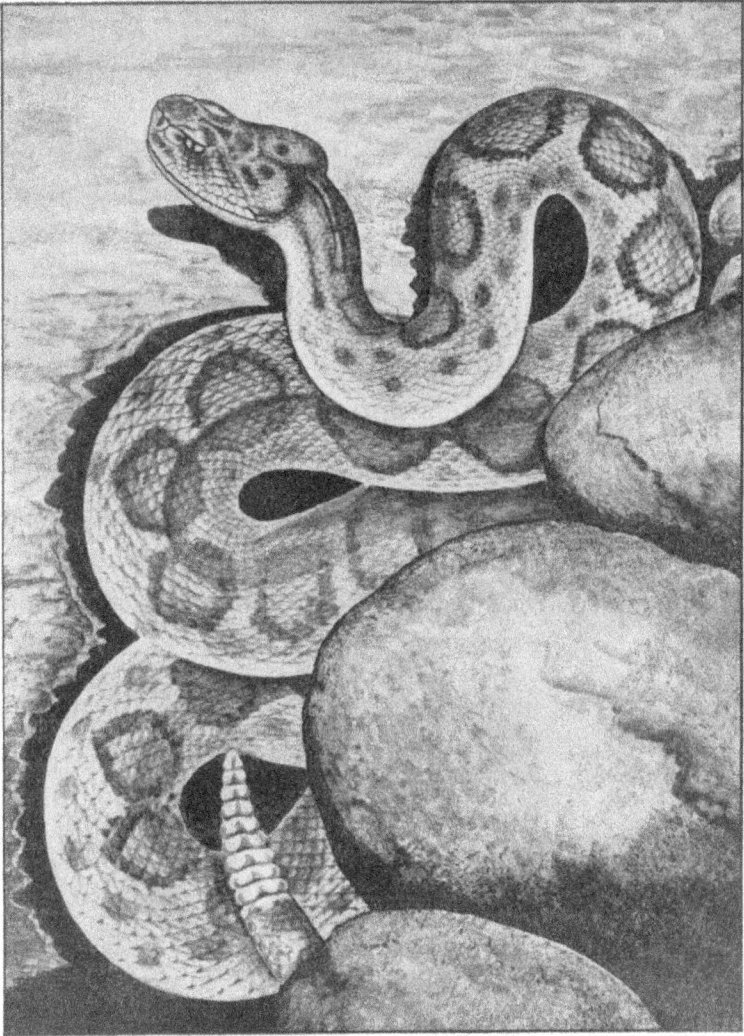

Atrox, the Desert Diamond Rattler

was not too bright, and there were long shadows from trees, shrubs, and giant cacti. Had Atrox thought much about it, he would have considered that this was the most enjoyable part of the day.

But Atrox did not do very much actual *thinking*; he got along mostly by *feeling*. He *sensed* that shade felt good on his skin, that ground squirrels felt good in his stomach, and that bright sunlight felt bad on his eyes. A feeling of fright or anger was enough to make him shake the rattle on the tip of his tail; and then, if something came near enough to disturb him further, Atrox used his poison fangs quite suddenly—certainly not waiting to do much thinking about it.

His poison was made in two glands, one in each side of his head, above the jaw. The poison glands were connected with two long, sharp, hollow teeth, or fangs. The poison, or venom, passed through these fangs when Atrox defended himself by biting.

Atrox was not really a quarrelsome snake. He did not fight unless he felt himself in danger. If animals let him alone, he let them alone too. That is, he did unless he was hungry. When he needed food he hunted for it; and when he caught a ground squirrel, or other prey, he used his fangs. The venom worked so quickly that the little animal did not even know that it was being swallowed.

It is this venom, of course, that makes a rattler a dangerous snake to meet suddenly and unexpectedly. A man, if bitten by one of these serpents, may die—or at least be made very ill. For this reason, people going through places where they expect to find a rattlesnake listen for the *whirr-rr-rr!* of his rattle. They take this sound as a warning not to come too near the creature that is making it.

The animals that heard Atrox's rattle most often were horses and cows that rambled through the canyon. Atrox might be lying quietly in a trail—and here would come a horse whose hoofs went *clop-clop* on the rocks. One thumping hoof could have killed Atrox. But did he wait to be thumped? Not at all! He coiled his body, held up the horny joints at the end of his tail, and shook them. His rattle made a queer, thin, buzzing sound that might mean to those who heard it, "Keep away! Don't touch me!" The horse always obeyed the rattle. He stopped as quickly as if there had been a rider on his back saying "Whoa!" and pulling on a rein. He snorted a few times and then went on with his thumping walk— not toward Atrox any more, but among the rocks near the trail.

At the time of which we are writing, Atrox was old enough to be about four feet long. Perhaps later he grew to be even longer. There was a row of dark brown blotches running along the middle of his back. These large blotches were somewhat diamond-shaped. There were also dark brown spots scattered over his sides. Underneath, he was yellowish white, and a pale yellow stripe ran down each side of his face. His tail was nearly white with several black ringlike bands around it.

There are rattlesnakes of several kinds that have diamond-shaped marks. There are rattlesnakes, too, that have their backs decorated with marks of a different shape. Sidewinder was one of these serpents.

SIDEWINDER

There are sidewinders who live near Red Racer's home but Sidewinder of this chapter dwelt far away from there. He stayed in the desert Chuck looked toward when he glanced down from his bare, hot ledge.

Sidewinder was a small rattlesnake, being only about fifteen inches long from the tip of his nose to the end of the rattle on his tail. His back was dull yellowish and dull grayish, and the blotches along the middle were light brown with paler places between them. His

Sidewinder was a "horned" rattlesnake.

colors were much like those of the sand on his desert home.

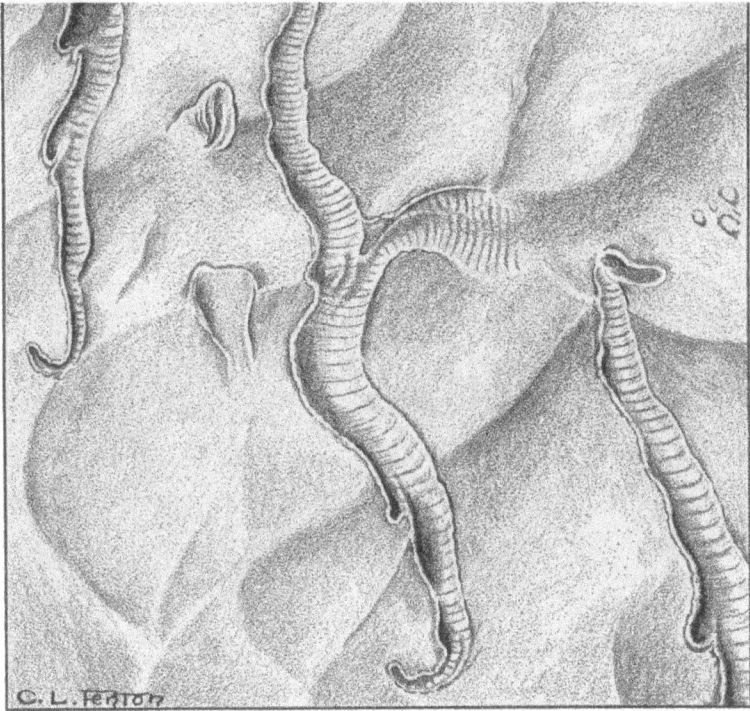

No serpent, except a sidewinder, could make a trail like this.

Though his colors were never bright, there were times when they were duller than usual. That was just before he molted the thin delicate skin that covered his scales. At such times even his eyes were dim and he was nearly blind. Before long, the old skin would split near his head and he would manage to wriggle out of it, turning it wrong side out like a stocking that is pulled off top first. All snakes shed their old skins now and then, and they look very fresh, indeed, after this performance.

Like Atrox, and other kinds of rattlesnakes, Side-winder had a heart-shaped head; but there were two things on his head that only sidewinders have. His upper eye shields were large and stiff, and they stuck up like horns. It is because of these "horns" that snakes of this sort are often called "horned rattlesnakes."

The queerest thing about Sidewinder was the way he traveled. To be sure, he could glide along like Atrox, and sometimes crawled that way. But if he was in a hurry he skipped over the loose sand in a strange sidewise manner. He would twist his head, move his tail, and then jerk his body from one place to another. While doing this he made wriggly tracks in the sand, each one showing the full length of his body. The head end of the track was curved much like the handle of some canes.

Like Atrox, Sidewinder would not go about during the hottest part of the day. Before it became too hot, he always crawled into a hole or lay in the shade of a bush, waiting for the air to grow cool and comfortable. At about five o'clock in the afternoon he would begin to hunt; and he might keep on hunting long after dark when the air was really chilly.

One evening, when Sidewinder first came out, he went to a creosote bush and lay there waiting for mice. After catching and eating the first mouse that came near him, he wriggled across the sand and captured a small lizard that seemed stiff and very sleepy.

Sidewinder still was hunting at ten o'clock that night when a coyote came rather near and sat down and began to howl. A moment later the coyote saw

Sidewinder move, so he went quickly to another place, where there were no rattlesnakes, before he finished his wolf song.

By midnight the desert was too cold even for Sidewinder. He stopped hunting, and when he came to some soft sand he wriggled his body into it, with his eyes and horns just at the surface. He did not suffer any, but he soon became too stiff and drowsy to move. He did not waken until well after sunrise.

CHAPTER XII

CHURCA, COCK OF THE DESERT

RAP, RAP, RAP—Churca was tapping with his bill. Later in his life he would use his bill for other work, but on that May day there was nothing in the world so important to him as tapping. There was no way for him to get out of his eggshell except to break it.

The nest that held him was made of sticks laid together rather loosely in a large cholla cactus. There was a lining with some dry grass, pieces of roots, the thin molted skin of a snake, and a few feathers.

Churca had five brothers and sisters in the nest—though, of course, he knew nothing about them. Two were still in their eggshells, but they were a week or so younger than Churca and so were not nearly ready to hatch. The other three youngsters, however, had hatched some time before, one being about half grown.

Birds of most kinds have babies that all hatch within a few hours of one another. The parents do not begin to brood the eggs until they are all laid. But Churca's parents were road runners, and road runners have ways

*The Road-Runner, or Cock of the Desert,
is the "state bird" of New Mexico.*

that are different from those of other birds. They have their own queer habits. Churca's mother did not lay her six eggs one each day for six days, and then begin to brood them. She began to brood her first egg soon after she laid it, and then she laid the others from time to time in a haphazard sort of way, with rather long waits between. Her mate took his turn at sitting on the eggs, so she did not have all the brooding to do.

After breaking his dull, yellowish white shell with the hard "egg tooth" at the tip of his upper bill, Churca sprawled in the nest without knowing what was going on there. He was hatched blind and naked, except for a few hairs on his dark body. He did not have open eyes and fluffy down like a baby chicken or duck.

Churca's father, Chaparral Cock, stood on the cactus branch at the edge of the nest and glanced at his new son. Two of his toes on each foot pointed forward and two backward. In that respect his feet were like those of a cuckoo. Indeed, he belonged to the Cuckoo Family, although, except for his feet, he did not look much like his relatives. A bird of this sort is sometimes called a "ground cuckoo."

Chaparral Cock had brought some food to the nest, but it was too big a mouthful for Churca to swallow. It was a lizard which he had caught and killed. He did not cut it into small bits. He thrust the whole lizard, head first, into the mouth of Churca's oldest brother. The lizard was eight or nine inches long, and the young bird could not swallow it all. The tail stuck out of his mouth—like a slender, pointed tongue five inches long.

*This is not a long tongue thrust out
from the young bird's mouth. It is a lizard's tail.*

Churca's brother did not choke. He sat quietly in the nest while he digested the lizard's head. Then he had room enough in his stomach for more lizard, so he swallowed some more with a gulp. In this way, little by little, the lizard slipped out of sight until even the tip of the tail was gone.

Churca's father and mother fed him grasshoppers and other insects and lizards. He grew, his eyes opened, and feathers covered his body. When he was old enough he left his nest and began to hunt for his own food. He learned how to chase grasshoppers and jump into the air to catch them when they started to fly; he had a jolly time picking up beetles; he felt pleased when he found a big juicy caterpillar; and while he was swallowing a lizard, he looked as cheerful as a boy with the kind of candy that is called an "all-day sucker"!

For a while Churca stayed in the neighborhood of his nest, where his parents could help take care of him. But grown-up road runners are not really sociable birds. They are hunters; and, like many other feathered and furry hunters, they go off alone or with their mates. So the time came when Churca left the home of his baby days and found a place where there were no other road runners. Here he could be a "cock of the desert," in his own hunting ground.

If you had not been very near him when he lifted the crest on his head, you might have thought that his eyes were blue and red; but these colors were really on a bare patch of skin behind each eye. Most of the feathers of his back and sides were dark and glossy with pale-colored edges. These feathers, with their mixed colors, made his coat streaked and dappled. His chest was lighter than his back, and the rest of his under feathers were plain grayish or buffy white. He was nearly two feet long from the tip of his beak to the tip of his tail. His tail measured twelve inches—or about half of his whole length. His legs were long and strong, or he could not have run so fast.

It was the way Churca ran that made him interesting

to some people who saw him on the desert. He often hunted along the side of a trail or a road, and sometimes a man on horseback or a driver of an automobile would chase him just for the fun of seeing how fast he could go. Churca, too, seemed to think it was fun to race. Nothing had ever caught him—so why should he be worried? He would put down his head and lower his tail and his "stream-lined" body would glide on ahead of the horse or the automobile as if he expected to win the race.

Churca could run easily at the rate of twenty miles an hour, but he was not stupid enough to try to stay in the road ahead of an automobile that came too near. If he were on a high place with a slope at one side, he might spread his wings and sail down the slope. He could use his wings on a down-hill flight, but he did not try to fly over level ground or up hill.

He did not need to fly to make his escape. He could dodge to one side without stopping. He turned by jerking his tail to one side, much as a man uses a rudder to steer a boat or an airplane or an airship. When he reached a clump of bushes he would hide there. It was not easy to see his striped and mottled body when he stood still.

It was even more fun to run after things he was chasing than to run away from things that were chasing him. Churca liked to eat any kind of game he could catch, and some of the snakes he followed were swift travelers. But he caught one now and then, and thus earned the name of "snake killer."

When Churca killed a slender snake that was not

more than a foot and a half long, he did not always bother to divide it. Often he just swallowed the head first and gulped down the rest of it, little by little, as soon as he had digested the part in his stomach. Rattlesnake meat was as delicious to him as any other kind. All the poison in the rattlesnake's poison glands did not disagree with him in the least.

Like all road runners, Churca took a great many baths; but none of them were water baths. Some were sun baths, during which he fluffed out his feathers to let them air in the warm, dry sunshine. The others were dust baths, when he wallowed in dry dust and shook it among his feathers.

It was neither feasting nor bathing that interested Churca one pleasant day in March. He felt more like singing than doing anything else just then. So he sang *"Whooo? Whooo?"* His voice sounded rather mournful, much like that of a dove singing the coo song; but Churca was not sad. He was really quite happy.

Churca could make other sounds besides his *whooo* song. When he was a very young baby in the nest, he had begged for something to eat by making a buzzing noise. He did this by rattling his beak very rapidly. Even after he was a grown bird he often rattled his beak as he went about the desert. He had a low *br-rr-rr* note, too.

But the day Churca sang *"Whooo? Whooo?"* he seemed to be calling. And far off on the desert another road runner heard and answered him. We may call this other road runner Miss Paisano. She liked the sound of Churca's voice and came into his desert home to meet him. When she came near enough, Churca did not always call so loudly. He sang a low really sweet *kook-kooo* song. Miss Paisano liked Churca as well as she did his music. The two road runners became mates and soon began to build a nest like the one Chaparral Cock and his mate had made—that one in which Churca had tapped while he was still inside his eggshell.

CHAPTER XIII

GUESTS OF THE YUCCA

You may remember reading, in the first chapter of this book, that yuccas are members of the Lily Family. A Joshua tree, which grows to be bigger than any other yucca in the United States, has a flower stalk only about a foot long at the tip of each branch. Yuccas of some other kinds, however, have flower stalks that may be more than fifteen feet long. Such a stalk grows straight up from the top of the part covered by the "bayonet" leaves. This flower stalk is tipped with many flowers grouped in a large loose cluster. There is also a yucca so short that its tuft of leaves spreads out on the ground. Its flower stalk is two or three feet long.

All the yuccas, whether of short or tall kinds, depend upon insects to help them so that they may have seeds that can grow.

You doubtless know that plants with flowers have parts called *stamens* and *pistils*. The pollen grains grow on the stamens. The seeds form inside the seed case which is part of the pistil; but they cannot live unless they are touched by pollen. Most flowers need to have pollen from another flower of the same kind to make their seeds grow.

How can pollen from one flower get to the sticky tip of a pistil in another flower? The wind carries pollen for grasses, sedges, oaks, pines, and for many other plants. The flowers of these plants are not showy or fragrant. They have great supplies of light pollen that can float off on the breezes.

Flowers with bright colors and attractive odors are visited by insects which carry their pollen for them. The insects, of course, do not know that they are helping the plants. They visit the flowers to get nectar or pollen, or both, for their own uses. Some of the dusty pollen, however, clings to the body of the insect until this visitor reaches another flower of the same kind and brushes against the sticky end of the pistil there. A pollen grain, left resting on the tip of a pistil, grows down inside the pistil until it reaches the seed case to help form a live seed.

Flower-visiting flies and beetles, as well as bees, butterflies, and moths act as pollen bearers for many flowers. The only insects that can help the yuccas, however, are the Pronuba moths. So we shall tell you the story of one of these insects, calling her Nuba for a short name.

NUBA

Nuba hatched from an egg that her mother had pushed into the young tender seed case of a yucca

*Nuba and her brothers and sisters lived
in these Yucca seed pods while they were young and hungry.*

flower. She was a very tiny larva and so delicate that she needed to be protected from hot sunshine and winds. She found her seed case the very best sort of nursery, for it sheltered her and held plenty of food. She was hungry soon after hatching. For her first meal she began to eat a juicy little seed that was just forming. This agreed with her and she continued to eat yucca seeds for about a month. It took her as long as that to eat ten seeds. There were about two hundred seeds in that seed pod, so the yucca plant could spare the few that Nuba needed.

After Nuba finished her tenth seed, she lost her appetite. She was not ill, but she was a full-grown larva and needed no more food. Although she had been busy eating most of that month, she did rest a few times while she molted her skin. Her complexion changed as she grew. At first she was nearly white, later she became yellowish, and now she was rather pink. The seed pod, which was small and tender when Nuba hatched from the egg, was now full sized and beginning to get hard. It was not too tough, however, for Nuba to make a hole in its side with her little caterpillar jaws. She wiggled out of the hole and dropped to the ground.

Nuba had never touched the ground before, of course, but she did not get lost or make any mistakes. She dug into the soil until she was several inches below the surface. Then she made a strong cocoon of silk. The silk came from her silk glands inside of her body, where it was stored in a liquid form. She squeezed it through an opening in her lower lip when she was ready to use it, and it hardened into a fiber as it came out. She spun her cocoon with this silken fiber.

The cocoon was a snug sleeping bag that covered her, head and all, but she did not smother in it. She did not need much air. She waited inside her cocoon during the fall and winter months and part of the spring. All this while she remained a pale little larva. Then, one spring day or night, something happened to her. She changed from a smooth larva into a pupa. After she became a pupa she rested a few more days inside her cocoon.

The pupa case had a sharp spine on its head and a lot of strong spoon-shaped spines on its back. Nuba used these spines as tools one day when she wriggled out of her cocoon and forced her way up through the sand to the surface of the ground.

While she was still inside her hard pupal skin, or case, something else happened to her. This time she changed into a little moth. The next thing she did was to split the hard case that covered her and creep out through the crack. At first her wings were too small and limp to fly with. She crawled up on some dry rubbish and clung there while her wings grew to full size and stiffened.

It was evening before Nuba felt like flying. The whole wide desert was open to her. Where should she go? Would her flight be a haphazard one—just anywhere at all? No, indeed! She had a pleasant guide. The yucca flowers were sending out an odor that was sweeter than anything else in the world to her. That scent was her guide. Nuba flew to one of these fragrant blossoms.

All about the desert that night and the next night and every night, as long as the yucca plants had fresh flowers, tiny little yucca moths, like Nuba, were seeking the blossoms. Among these moths was one who became Nuba's mate. He found her waiting in a yucca blossom.

Nuba rested in the daytime, but she was very busy at night. Soon after dark she climbed to the top of a stamen, where she found some pollen.

She uncoiled her long tongue and reached it over to the farther edge of the stamen to help her cling there while she worked. On the under side of her head, near the base of her tongue, she had a pair of little things that she did not use for mouth parts. She could curve these and use them like slender arms to help her collect and hold the pollen. She packed all the pollen she could get from one stamen into a little mass. Then she climbed to the top of another stamen in the same blossom and added more pollen to her mass. When she had a load of pollen bigger than her head, she flew away to another yucca blossom.

The first thing Nuba did when she reached this new flower was to find a pistil. She had an egg-laying tool at the tail end of her body. It was stiff and sharp like a slender little knife. She pressed the end of this tool into the tender part of the pistil, which would grow into the seed pod. As soon as she had reached her tool in far enough she laid an egg.

Her next job was to climb to the top of the pistil and thrust in some of the pollen she was carrying. She poked it into the opening at the tip of the pistil. This pollen

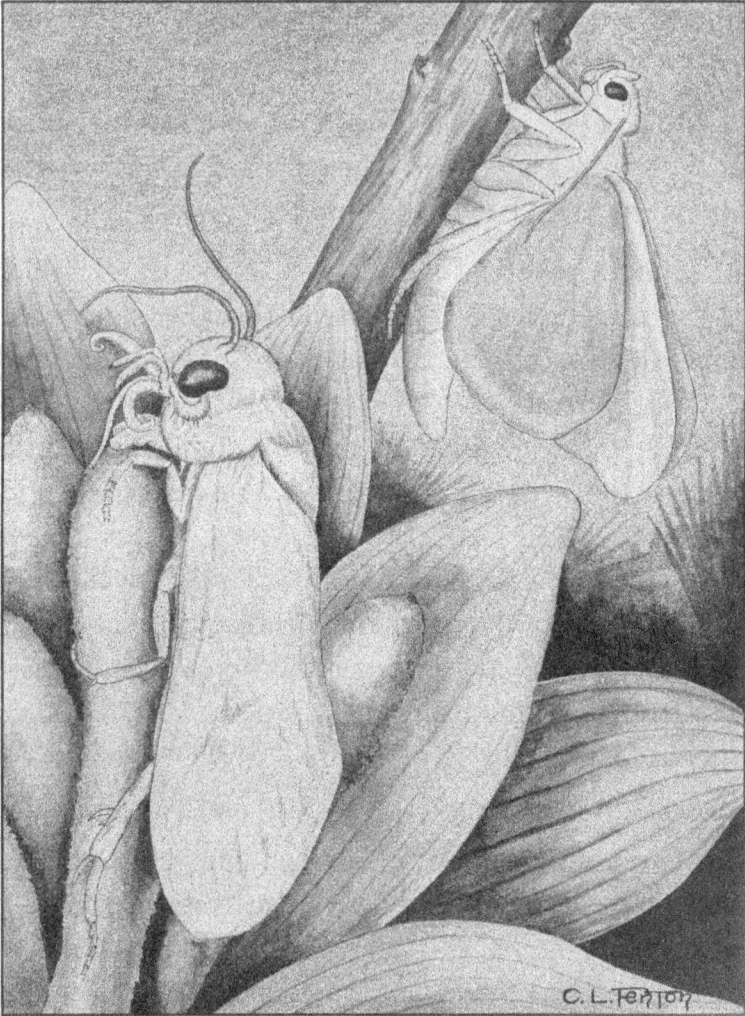

*Nuba was ready to gather pollen from the tip
of a stamen in a yucca blossom.*

would make the seeds able to live and grow. Nuba's baby larva, which would hatch from the egg she had just laid, would eat about ten of these seeds. Other seeds would be left to get ripe. The pod would then open and the seeds would be sown by the wind. So Nuba helped the yucca plant at the same time she was helping her baby. She gathered several loads of pollen from stamens and put it into pistils, and she laid quite a number of eggs. Her nights, as you may see, were not idle.

When Nuba folded her wings and rested, she looked like an all-white moth, for the upper side of her front wings was white. When she spread her wings and showed all four of them, she was white and black, for her hind wings were slaty gray or nearly black.

DOXUS

Nuba was not the only tiny moth who rested in yucca blossoms by day and laid eggs at night. Doxus might often be found in the same flowers. (This name really is *Prodoxus*, but perhaps you will not object to our nickname.)

The wings of Doxus were much like those of Nuba—showing only white when folded, but showing white and slaty black when she flew. Indeed, moths of these two kinds look so much alike that people have often mistaken one for the other. A *Prodoxus* moth is sometimes called a "bogus yucca moth."

Though Doxus looked so much like Nuba, her habits were different. She did not gather balls of yucca pollen and poke them into yucca pistils. She could not do that because she did not have the right sort of tools to use in collecting pollen in this way. And when she laid her eggs she did not put them into the young yucca seed pods.

At night when Doxus was ready to lay her eggs, she left the yucca blossom and flew to the big tall flower stalk. This stalk was green and, at that time of year, was not very hard and tough. Doxus had a good egg-laying tool—a bit stronger even than Nuba's. She thrust it into the green stalk and laid an egg. Then she moved to a near-by spot and pushed a second egg into the same stalk. She kept working in this way until she was rid of all her eggs.

Each baby that hatched from these eggs was a tiny white larva. We may as well call one of them young Pro. Pro had no legs at all and looked like a helpless little grub. She had perfectly good jaws, however, and ate all she wanted of the juicy tender yucca stalk, making a little tunnel as she chewed her way along.

By the time Pro was a full-sized larva, her tunnel had reached nearly to the surface of the stalk. So she nibbled a circle for a door. She did not chew quite through to the outside, so her circle stayed shut like a closed lid or trap door.

Pro, then, did not drop to the ground as Nuba did. She remained in her tunnel and spun her silk and wove her cocoon there. She slept in her cocoon that fall and winter and part of the next spring. Then, when it was the proper time, she changed into a pupa with a brown case.

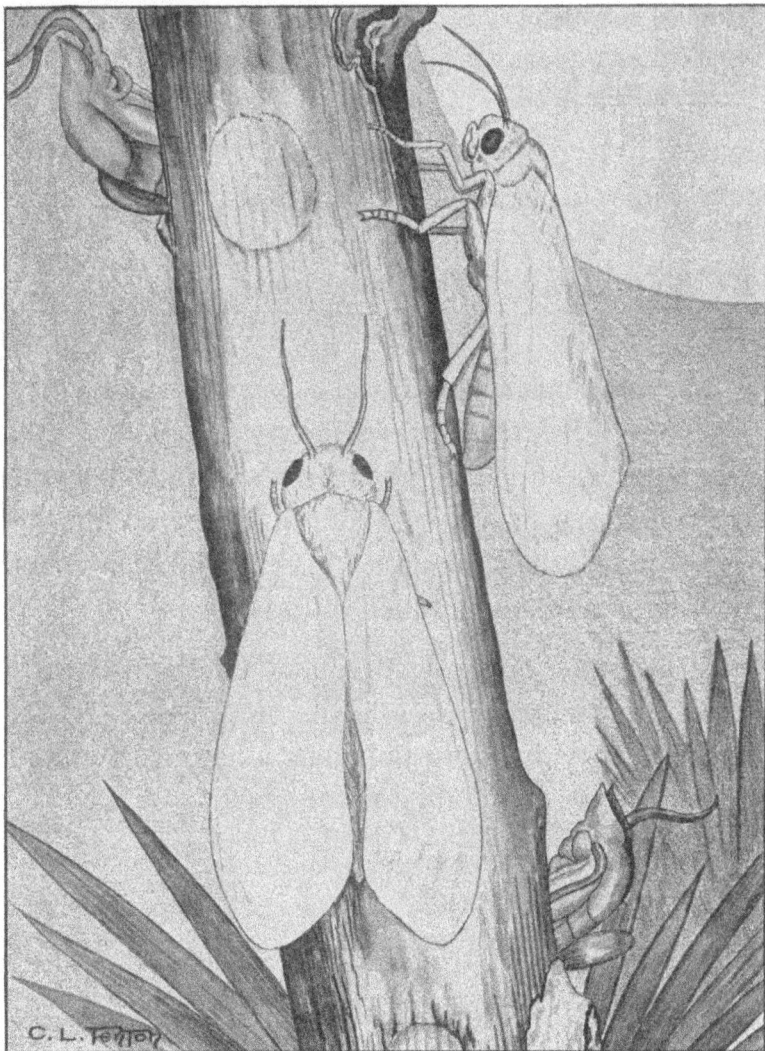

Two "Bogus Yucca Moths" and Their Empty Pupa Cases

This pupa was not like Nuba's, for it had no spines on its back to dig with. Pro did not need to dig in order to escape. All she needed to do was to open the circular door of her tunnel. She had the right sort of tool for this—a strong prong on the head end of the pupa. She knocked on the inside of her door with this tool and butted it open. She went part way out, but not all the way. There she waited until she was ready to break the case; then she left it. Of course, by that time, she was a moth with wings partly white and partly slaty black like those of her mother.

About the same time all of Pro's brothers and sisters came out of their trap doors in the yucca stalk. The stalk was not green and juicy now. It was a hard tough wood. They could not have got out of it if it were not for the doorways they had prepared while the stalk was tender and while they still had their biting jaws.

These little "bogus yucca moths" left that old dried stalk and fluttered forth into the moonlight. And on their way they met some of Nuba's sons and daughters who were also taking their first flight.

A BOOK LIST

IN connection with certain subjects in *Desert Neighbors*, references have been made to chapters or articles in the following books:

First Lessons in Nature Study by Edith M. Patch

Mountain Neighbors by Edith M. Patch and Carroll Lane Fenton

Nature Magazine, Vol 9, 1927

The Work of Scientists by Edith M. Patch and Carroll Lane Fenton

www.ingramcontent.com/pod-product-compliance
Lightning Source LLC
Chambersburg PA
CBHW031850090426
42741CB00005B/435